CHARLES VANCE

Ethical Hacking Volume 1: InfoSec

Concepts, Controls, and Laws

Contents

Preface

In today's world, information security is more important than ever before. With the increasing reliance on digital technology, businesses and individuals face a growing number of threats to their sensitive information. Cyberattacks, data breaches, and hacking attempts have become commonplace, and the consequences of a security breach can be devastating.

This book aims to provide an overview of information security and its various aspects. The book is intended for anyone who wants to gain a basic understanding of information security, from students to professionals in the field. It is also useful for anyone who wants to learn about ethical hacking and best practices for securing information systems.

The book begins with an introduction to information security and its importance in today's digital world. It then covers different types of information security threats, including cyberattacks and data breaches, and their impact on individuals and organizations. The goals of information security, including confidentiality, integrity, and availability, are also discussed.

This is volume 1 of a 21 volume set designed to provide a comprehensive understanding of the concepts, techniques, tools, and countermeasures related to information security and ethical hacking. Each volume is tailored to cover a specific topic related to the CEH exam and provides in-depth knowledge and practical skills required to pass the certification exam.

Volume 1: InfoSec: Concepts, Controls, and Laws

This volume provides an overview of information security concepts, including security models, policies, standards, and regulations. It covers the legal and ethical aspects of information security, including privacy and data protection laws, and the role of security controls in maintaining the confidentiality, integrity, and availability of information.

Volume 2: Footprinting: Techniques and Countermeasures

This volume covers the techniques and tools used to gather information about a target system or network, including passive and active reconnaissance, social engineering, and open-source intelligence. It also provides countermeasures to prevent and detect footprinting attacks.

Volume 3: Network Scanning Concepts: A Comprehensive Guide to Network Security

This volume covers the concepts and tools used to scan a network for vulnerabilities, including port scanning, service identification, and vulnerability scanning. It also provides an overview of network security controls and countermeasures.

Volume 4: Mastering Enumeration Techniques: Tools and Countermeasures for Network Reconnaissance

This volume covers the techniques and tools used to gather detailed information about a target system or network, including user and group enumeration, network shares, and password policies. It also provides countermeasures to prevent and detect enumeration attacks.

Volume 5: Vulnerability Assessment: Concepts, Tools, and Reports

This volume covers the concepts and tools used to identify and assess vulnerabilities in a system or network, including vulnerability scanning, penetration testing, and risk assessment. It also provides an overview of vulnerability reporting and management.

Volume 6: Mastering System Hacking: From Access to Execution

This volume covers the techniques and tools used to gain unauthorized access to a system, escalate privileges, and execute malicious code. It also provides countermeasures to prevent and detect system hacking attacks.

Volume 7: Malware Concepts: Understanding the Types and Countermeasures

This volume covers the types of malware, including viruses, worms, Trojans, and ransomware, and their characteristics, behavior, and propagation methods. It also provides countermeasures to prevent and detect malware attacks.

Volume 8: Understanding Sniffing Techniques and Countermeasures

This volume covers the techniques and tools used to intercept and analyze network traffic, including packet sniffing, ARP spoofing, and DNS poisoning. It also provides countermeasures to prevent and detect sniffing attacks.

Volume 9: Understanding Social Engineering Concepts: Techniques, Threats, and Countermeasures

This volume covers the techniques and tools used to manipulate people to divulge confidential information, including phishing, pretexting, and baiting. It also provides countermeasures to prevent and detect social engineering attacks.

Volume 10: Understanding DoS/DDoS Attacks and How to Protect Against Them

This volume covers the types of Denial-of-Service (DoS) and Distributed Denial-of-Service (DDoS) attacks and their characteristics, behavior, and impact. It also provides countermeasures to prevent and mitigate DoS/DDoS attacks.

Volume 11: Understanding Session Hijacking: Concepts, Tools, and Countermeasures

This volume covers the techniques and tools used to hijack user sessions and gain unauthorized access to a system or network, including session fixation, session prediction, and session hijacking. It also provides countermeasures to prevent and detect session hijacking attacks.

Volume 12: Understanding IDS, IPS, Firewall, and Honeypot Concepts

This volume covers the concepts and functions of Intrusion Detection Systems (IDS),Intrusion Prevention Systems (IPS), firewalls, and honeypots. It explains how these technologies work and how they can be used to detect, prevent, and respond to network attacks.

Volume 13: Hacking Web Servers: Understanding Attacks and Countermeasures

This volume covers the techniques and tools used to exploit vulnerabilities in web servers, including web application attacks, server misconfigurations, and file inclusion vulnerabilities. It also provides countermeasures to prevent and detect web server attacks.

Volume 14: Hacking Web Applications: A Comprehensive Guide

This volume covers the techniques and tools used to exploit vulnerabilities in web applications, including SQL injection, Cross-Site Scripting (XSS), and Cross-Site Request Forgery (CSRF). It also provides countermeasures to prevent and detect web application attacks.

Volume 15: Understanding SQL Injection: Types, Methodology, Tools, Evasion Techniques, and Countermeasures

This volume covers the techniques and tools used to exploit SQL injection vulnerabilities in web applications, including SQL syntax, injection methods, and evasion techniques. It also provides countermeasures to prevent and detect SQL injection attacks.

Volume 16: Hacking Wireless Networks: Understanding Concepts, Encryption, Threats, Methodology, and Countermeasures

This volume covers the concepts, encryption methods, and threats related to wireless networks, including Wi-Fi, Bluetooth, and ZigBee. It also covers the methodology and tools used to hack wireless networks and provides countermeasures to prevent and detect wireless attacks.

Volume 17: Hacking Mobile Platforms: A Comprehensive Guide to Securing Your Mobile Device

This volume covers the techniques and tools used to exploit vulnerabilities in mobile platforms, including Android and iOS. It also covers the methodology and countermeasures to prevent and detect mobile platform attacks.

Volume 18: IoT and OT Hacking: Understanding Concepts, Attacks, Methodologies, Tools, and Countermeasures

This volume covers the concepts, attacks, methodologies, and tools used to exploit vulnerabilities in Internet of Things (IoT) and Operational Technology (OT) devices. It also provides countermeasures to prevent and detect IoT and OT attacks.

Volume 19: A Comprehensive Overview of Cloud Computing and Security

This volume covers the concepts and technologies related to cloud computing, including Infrastructure-as-a-Service (IaaS), Platform-as-a-Service (PaaS), and Software-as-a-Service (SaaS). It also covers the security risks and countermeasures related to cloud computing.

Volume 20: Cryptography: The Complete Guide to Encryption and Decryption

This volume covers the concepts and technologies related to cryptography, including symmetric and asymmetric encryption, digital signatures, and hash functions. It also covers the implementation and best practices of cryptography in information security.

Volume 21: CEH: A Comprehensive Guide to Ace Your Certified Ethical Hacker Exam

This volume provides a comprehensive guide to prepare for the Certified Ethical Hacker (CEH) certification exam. It covers the exam objectives, study tips, practice questions, and exam-taking strategies. It also includes a summary of the key concepts and techniques covered in the previous volumes.

1

Information Security Overview

There are several types of information security threats that can pose a risk to organizations and individuals alike. Here are some common examples:

1. Malware: Malware is any malicious software that is designed to infiltrate, damage or disrupt computer systems. Examples include viruses, Trojans, worms, and ransomware.
2. Phishing: Phishing is a type of social engineering attack that involves the use of fraudulent emails or messages to trick individuals into providing sensitive information or clicking on malicious links.
3. Insider threats: Insider threats refer to individuals within an organization who intentionally or unintentionally pose a security risk. This can include employees, contractors, or partners who have access to sensitive data.
4. Denial of Service (DoS) attacks: A DoS attack is designed to overwhelm a system or network with traffic or requests, causing it to become unavailable or unresponsive.

5. Advanced Persistent Threats (APTs): APTs are long-term, targeted attacks that are designed to gain access to sensitive data or systems over a period of time. They often involve multiple stages and sophisticated techniques.
6. Man-in-the-middle (MitM) attacks: MitM attacks involve intercepting communication between two parties in order to steal data or insert malicious code.
7. Physical attacks: Physical attacks involve physically accessing computer systems, networks or devices in order to steal or damage data.
8. Data breaches: A data breach is an incident in which sensitive, protected or confidential data is accessed or disclosed without authorization.

These are just a few examples of the types of information security threats that individuals and organizations face. It's important to be aware of these threats and take appropriate measures to protect against them.

Information Security Threats

Information security threats can have a significant impact on both individuals and organizations. Here are some of the potential consequences:

1. Financial loss: Many information security threats, such as ransomware attacks or phishing scams, can result in financial loss for individuals or organizations. For example, a ransomware attack can lock an organization out of its own data until a ransom is paid, while a phishing scam can result in stolen credit card or banking information.

2. Reputation damage: If an organization suffers a data breach or other security incident, it can damage the organization's reputation and erode trust with customers or stakeholders. This can have long-term consequences for the organization's brand and financial performance.

3. Legal and regulatory penalties: Depending on the nature of the security incident, individuals or organizations may be subject to legal and regulatory penalties. For example, organizations may be fined for violating data protection laws, while individuals may face criminal charges for hacking or other cybercrimes.

4. Disruption of operations: Many information security threats can disrupt an organization's operations, whether through a denial of service attack or a malware infection that renders critical systems unusable. This can result in lost productivity and revenue, as well as damage to the organization's reputation.

5. Personal harm: In some cases, information security threats can directly harm individuals, such as in the case of identity theft or medical record breaches. This can result in financial loss, emotional distress, and other negative impacts.

Overall, information security threats can have wide-ranging and long-lasting impacts on both individuals and organizations. It is important to take proactive steps to protect against these threats, including implementing strong security protocols and regularly training employees on best practices.

Goals of Information Security (CIA Triad)

The goals of information security are often summarized using the CIA triad, which stands for Confidentiality, Integrity, and Availability. These three goals help to guide information security practices and ensure that data is protected from a variety of threats.

1. Confidentiality: Confidentiality refers to the protection of sensitive information from unauthorized access or disclosure. This includes personal data, financial information, and intellectual property. The goal is to ensure that only authorized users have access to this information, and that it is not disclosed to unauthorized parties. Confidentiality is often achieved through the use of encryption, access controls, and other security measures.

2. Integrity: Integrity refers to the protection of data from unauthorized modification, deletion, or corruption. This includes ensuring that data is accurate, complete, and trustworthy. The goal is to ensure that data remains unchanged throughout its lifecycle and that any changes are made by authorized users. Integrity is often achieved through the use of data backups, checksums, and other verification techniques.

3. Availability: Availability refers to the assurance that data and systems are available to authorized users when needed. This includes ensuring that systems are up and running, and that data is accessible to those who need it. The goal is to prevent downtime or disruptions that could impact productivity or operations. Availability is often achieved through the use of redundancy, failover mechanisms, and

disaster recovery planning.

Overall, the CIA triad provides a framework for information security that is focused on protecting data from a variety of threats. By ensuring that data is confidential, trustworthy, and available, organizations can maintain the confidentiality, integrity, and availability of their most sensitive information.

Discussion

Information security threats pose a significant risk to individuals and organizations, and it is important to be aware of common threats and take steps to protect against them. The most common types of information security threats include malware, phishing, insider threats, denial of service (DoS) attacks, advanced persistent threats (APTs), man-in-the-middle (MitM) attacks, physical attacks, and data breaches.

To protect against these threats, organizations can implement strong security protocols, such as access controls, encryption, and regular security training for employees. They can also use intrusion detection and prevention systems, firewalls, and other tools to monitor and protect their networks and systems. It is important for individuals to also take steps to protect themselves from information security threats, including being vigilant about phishing scams, using strong passwords and two-factor authentication, keeping software up-to-date, and avoiding public Wi-Fi networks when accessing sensitive data.

A data breach can have significant consequences, including financial loss, reputation damage, legal and regulatory penalties, disruption of operations, and personal harm to individuals whose data has been exposed. Insider threats can also have a significant impact on organizations, including loss of intellectual property, reputational damage, financial loss, and legal and regulatory penalties.

Emerging information security threats include artificial intelligence (AI)-powered attacks, ransomware-as-a-service (RaaS), and attacks targeting Internet of Things (IoT) devices. Organizations can balance the need for data security with the need for data accessibility by implementing strong access controls, using encryption and other security measures to protect sensitive data, and providing access to data only to those who need it.

Governments play a role in protecting against information security threats by passing and enforcing data protection laws, sharing threat intelligence with other countries and organizations, and investing in cybersecurity research and development. Organizations can prepare for a cybersecurity incident by developing a comprehensive incident response plan, conducting regular security assessments and penetration testing, and providing regular security training to employees.

Finally, the use of personal data for cybersecurity purposes raises ethical concerns, including issues of privacy, consent, and the potential for misuse of personal data. It is important for organizations to use personal data responsibly and transparently, and to comply with relevant data protection laws and regulations. By taking these steps, individuals and organizations can help protect against information security threats and safeguard sensitive data.

It is also important for organizations to stay up-to-date with the latest cybersecurity trends and best practices in order to protect against emerging threats. This includes staying current with software and hardware updates, monitoring and analyzing network traffic for potential threats, and conducting regular security audits.

Another important aspect of information security is incident response planning. Organizations should have a comprehensive plan in place to quickly and effectively respond to a cybersecurity incident. This plan should include procedures for detecting, containing, and mitigating the impact of a breach, as well as strategies for communicating with stakeholders, law enforcement, and other relevant parties.

In addition to protecting against external threats, organizations must also be aware of the risks posed by internal threats. Insider threats can come from employees, contractors, or other trusted parties who have access to sensitive information. These threats can include intentional or unintentional data breaches, theft of intellectual property, or other malicious activities. Organizations should have policies and procedures in place to prevent, detect, and respond to insider threats.

Overall, information security threats continue to evolve and become more sophisticated, requiring organizations to remain vigilant and proactive in protecting sensitive data. By implementing strong security protocols, staying up-to-date with the latest trends and best practices, and planning for potential incidents, organizations can help minimize the risks posed by information security threats and safeguard their most valuable assets.

Quiz (Solutions in Appendix)

1. What are the most common types of information security threats?
2. How can organizations protect against information security threats?
3. What are the potential consequences of a data breach?
4. What is the impact of insider threats on organizations?
5. How can individuals protect themselves from information security threats?
6. What are some emerging information security threats?
7. How can organizations balance the need for data security with the need for data accessibility?
8. What is the role of government in protecting against information security threats?
9. How can organizations prepare for a cybersecurity incident?
10. What are the ethical implications of using personal data for cybersecurity purposes?

2

Cyber Kill Chain Concepts

The Cyber Kill Chain is a framework that describes the stages of a cyber attack, from the initial reconnaissance to the final exfiltration of data. It was first introduced by Lockheed Martin in 2011 as a way to help organizations understand and prevent advanced cyber threats.

The seven stages of the Cyber Kill Chain are:

1. Reconnaissance: The attacker gathers information about the target system, including its vulnerabilities and possible attack vectors.
2. Weaponization: The attacker creates a weapon, such as malware or a phishing email, that will be used to exploit the target system.
3. Delivery: The attacker delivers the weapon to the target system, typically through a phishing email or other social engineering tactics.
4. Exploitation: The weapon is used to exploit a vulnerability in the target system, giving the attacker access to the

system.

5. Installation: The attacker installs a backdoor or other means of maintaining access to the target system.

6. Command and Control: The attacker establishes a command and control channel to the compromised system, allowing them to control it remotely.

7. Actions on Objectives: The attacker carries out their ultimate goal, such as stealing sensitive data, disrupting services, or damaging the system.

The Cyber Kill Chain model is useful for understanding the different stages of a cyber attack and for developing defenses that can detect and disrupt attacks at various stages of the chain. By breaking down the attack process into discrete stages, defenders can identify weaknesses and vulnerabilities in their defenses and develop strategies for preventing, detecting, and responding to attacks.

Reconnaissance: Stage 1

Reconnaissance is the first stage of the Cyber Kill Chain, where an attacker gathers information about the target system, network, or organization. This information can be collected through various means, including:

1. Open-source intelligence (OSINT): Publicly available information on the target, such as information available on social media platforms, websites, and other online resources.

2. Active scanning: The attacker uses tools to scan the target system or network for vulnerabilities, open ports, and

other information.

3. Social engineering: The attacker may contact employees or other individuals within the target organization, posing as a trustworthy person, to gain access to sensitive information.

4. Physical reconnaissance: The attacker may physically visit the target organization's premises or gather information about the target system through observation.

The goal of reconnaissance is to gather as much information as possible about the target system or organization to identify vulnerabilities that can be exploited later in the attack. This information can include IP addresses, domain names, email addresses, employee names, job titles, software and hardware in use, network architecture, and more. The reconnaissance stage is critical because it allows the attacker to determine the best approach to launch a successful attack and to avoid detection. Defenses against reconnaissance include implementing access controls, monitoring for suspicious activity, and limiting the amount of information available publicly about the organization.

Weaponization: Stage 2

Weaponization is the second stage of the Cyber Kill Chain, where an attacker creates a weapon or tool that will be used to exploit the target system. This weapon can take different forms, including malware, exploit code, or a phishing email.

Malware is a type of software that is designed to infiltrate a target system and perform malicious actions. Malware can take many forms, including viruses, trojans, worms, and ran-somware. Once installed on the target system, malware can steal data, disrupt services, or provide the attacker with access to the system.

Exploit code is a tool that is designed to exploit a specific vulnerability in a target system. Once the vulnerability is exploited, the attacker gains access to the system, which can then be used to steal data, disrupt services, or perform other malicious actions.

Phishing emails are emails that are designed to trick the re-cipient into clicking on a link or opening an attachment that contains malware or exploit code. Phishing emails often appear to come from a legitimate source, such as a trusted company or individual, and may use social engineering tactics to convince the recipient to take the desired action.

The goal of the weaponization stage is to create a tool that can successfully exploit the vulnerabilities identified during the reconnaissance stage. Defenses against weaponization include implementing security controls, such as antivirus software and email filters, that can detect and block malware and exploit code, and providing security awareness training to employees to help them identify and avoid phishing emails.

Delivery: Stage 3

Delivery is the third stage of the Cyber Kill Chain, where an attacker delivers the weapon or tool created in the previous stage to the target system. Delivery can take many forms, including:

12

1. Email: The attacker sends a phishing email to the target, containing a link or attachment that will install the weapon or tool on the target system when clicked or opened.
2. Social media: The attacker may use social media platforms to send a message containing a link or attachment that will install the weapon or tool on the target system.
3. Drive-by download: The attacker may place the weapon or tool on a website, and when the target visits the website, the weapon or tool is automatically downloaded and installed.
4. Physical media: The attacker may use a USB drive or other physical media to deliver the weapon or tool to the target system.

The delivery stage is critical because it determines whether the weapon or tool will successfully reach the target system and be installed. Defenses against delivery include implementing security controls, such as email filters, web filters, and antivirus software, that can detect and block malicious content, and providing security awareness training to employees to help them identify and avoid phishing emails and other forms of social engineering.

Exploitation: Stage 4

Exploitation is the fourth stage of the Cyber Kill Chain, where an attacker uses the weapon or tool to exploit a vulnerability in the target system. Once the weapon or tool has been delivered, the attacker will attempt to use it to gain access to the target system. This can take various forms, including:

1. Social engineering: The attacker may trick the target into running the weapon or tool by posing as a trusted source or using other social engineering tactics.
2. Software vulnerabilities: The attacker may use the weapon or tool to exploit a vulnerability in software or firmware on the target system.
3. Hardware vulnerabilities: The attacker may use the weapon or tool to exploit a vulnerability in hardware on the target system, such as a USB port or network interface card.

Once the attacker has successfully exploited a vulnerability, they can gain access to the target system and perform further malicious actions, such as stealing data, installing backdoors or other tools, or launching attacks on other systems. Defenses against exploitation include implementing security controls, such as patching vulnerabilities, disabling unnecessary services, and using network segmentation to limit the attacker's access to sensitive systems.

Installation: Stage 5

Installation is the fifth stage of the Cyber Kill Chain, where an attacker installs a persistent presence on the target system. Once the attacker has successfully exploited a vulnerability and gained access to the target system, they will often attempt to install additional tools or backdoors to maintain access to the system even if the original entry point is discovered and closed. The installation can take various forms, including:

1. Backdoors: The attacker may install a backdoor on the

target system that allows them to regain access to the system at a later time. The backdoor may be hidden or disguised to avoid detection.

2. Rootkits: The attacker may install a rootkit on the target system that allows them to maintain access to the system while hiding their presence from system administrators and security tools.

3. Persistence mechanisms: The attacker may install persistence mechanisms on the target system that allow their tools or backdoors to remain active even after the system is rebooted.

The installation stage is critical because it allows the attacker to maintain access to the target system and continue to carry out their objectives. Defenses against installation include implementing security controls, such as intrusion detection systems and endpoint protection solutions, that can detect and block malicious activity, and regularly monitoring systems for suspicious behavior.

Command and Control: Stage 6

Command and Control (C2) is the sixth stage of the Cyber Kill Chain, where an attacker establishes a communication channel to control the compromised system remotely. Once the attacker has successfully installed a persistent presence on the target system, they will often attempt to establish a C2 channel to issue commands and control the compromised system. This can take various forms, including:

1. Command-and-control servers: The attacker may set up

a command-and-control server that the compromised system connects to in order to receive commands and transmit data.

2. Peer-to-peer networks: The attacker may use a peer-to-peer network to establish communication between the compromised system and other systems under the attacker's control.

3. Hidden services: The attacker may use hidden services to establish a communication channel that is difficult to detect and block.

Once the attacker has established a C2 channel, they can use it to issue commands to the compromised system, such as stealing data, installing additional tools, or launching attacks on other systems. Defenses against C2 include implementing security controls, such as firewalls and intrusion detection systems, that can detect and block outbound traffic to known C2 servers, and monitoring systems for suspicious activity.

Actions on Objectives: Stage 7

Actions on Objectives is the final stage of the Cyber Kill Chain, where the attacker carries out their ultimate goal, which may include stealing sensitive data, disrupting services, or damaging the target system. The attacker may take various steps to achieve their objectives, including:

1. Data exfiltration: The attacker may attempt to steal sensitive data from the target system, such as personal information, financial data, or intellectual property.

2. Disruption of services: The attacker may attempt to disrupt

the services or operations of the target system, such as by launching a distributed denial-of-service (DDoS) attack or by altering or deleting data.

3. Persistence: The attacker may attempt to maintain access to the target system by installing additional backdoors or tools, or by creating new accounts or users with elevated privileges.

4. Covering tracks: The attacker may attempt to cover their tracks by deleting logs or other evidence of their presence on the target system.

The goal of the Actions on Objectives stage is to achieve the attacker's ultimate objective, whether that is stealing data, disrupting services, or causing other damage. Defenses against Actions on Objectives include implementing security controls, such as data loss prevention and backup and recovery solutions, that can protect data and services from unauthorized access or damage, and conducting regular security assessments and penetration testing to identify and address vulnerabilities in the system.

Real world Examples

Many real-world cyber attacks follow the Cyber Kill Chain model. Here are a few examples:

1. Stuxnet: Stuxnet was a sophisticated malware attack that targeted Iran's nuclear program. The attack followed the Cyber Kill Chain, starting with reconnaissance to identify vulnerabilities in the target system, followed by weaponization of the malware, delivery via infected

USB drives, exploitation of a vulnerability in the target system, installation of a backdoor and a rootkit, command and control through servers outside the target system, and ultimately, the destruction of centrifuges used in the Iranian nuclear program.

2. WannaCry: WannaCry was a ransomware attack that affected hundreds of thousands of computers around the world. The attack followed the Cyber Kill Chain, starting with reconnaissance to identify vulnerable systems, followed by weaponization of the ransomware, delivery through a phishing email campaign, exploitation of a vulnerability in Microsoft Windows, installation of the ransomware, command and control through a hardcoded domain, and ultimately, the encryption of data and a ransom demand.

3. Target breach: In 2013, Target suffered a major data breach that affected over 40 million credit and debit card accounts. The attack followed the Cyber Kill Chain, starting with reconnaissance to identify vulnerabilities in Target's payment system, followed by weaponization of malware, delivery through a phishing email campaign to a third-party vendor, exploitation of a vulnerability in the vendor's system, installation of malware on Target's payment system, command and control through an external server, and ultimately, the exfiltration of payment data.

These are just a few examples, but many other cyber attacks follow the Cyber Kill Chain model to some extent. Understanding the Cyber Kill Chain can help organizations develop defenses and strategies to detect and disrupt attacks at various stages of the chain.

Discussion

Detecting and preventing attacks that do not follow the traditional Cyber Kill Chain model can be a challenging task for organizations. One solution proposed is implementing machine learning algorithms and behavioral analysis tools that can detect unusual activity and identify anomalies that may indicate an attack.

Individuals can play an important role in preventing cyber attacks that target their personal devices and data. Educating individuals about cyber hygiene and best practices, such as using strong passwords, enabling two-factor authentication, and avoiding suspicious links and attachments, is one of the suggested solutions.

Social engineering attacks pose a significant threat to organizations, and it is important to ensure that employees are aware of these threats and how to recognize and avoid them. Providing regular security awareness training that includes simulated phishing attacks and other social engineering scenarios is one solution suggested to improve employee awareness of these threats.

Insider threats are a significant concern for organizations, as employees can either intentionally or unintentionally compromise security. One solution proposed to prevent such threats is to implement access controls, monitoring tools, and background checks to prevent unauthorized access and detect suspicious activity.

Implementing a security operations center (SOC) and incident response team can help organizations improve incident response and reduce the time to detect and respond to cyber attacks. These teams can quickly detect and respond to security incidents, minimizing the damage caused by the attack.

Threat intelligence feeds can provide real-time information about emerging threats and vulnerabilities, helping organizations to identify and prevent cyber attacks before they happen. By implementing threat intelligence, organizations can stay ahead of emerging threats and vulnerabilities and take appropriate actions to prevent attacks.

Regular security assessments and penetration testing can help organizations ensure that their security controls are effective and up-to-date. By identifying vulnerabilities and assessing the effectiveness of security controls, organizations can take steps to improve their security posture and minimize the risk of cyber attacks.

Third-party risk management programs can help organizations ensure that their supply chain partners and third-party vendors are not compromising their security. These programs can include due diligence and ongoing monitoring of supply chain partners and vendors to minimize the risk of cyber attacks.

Implementing strong data encryption, access controls, and data loss prevention tools can help organizations prevent data exfiltration and ensure the security of their sensitive data, even in the event of a successful cyber attack. By encrypting sensitive data and limiting access to it, organizations can minimize the risk of data loss or theft.

Governments and international organizations can play an important role in promoting global cybersecurity and preventing cyber attacks on critical infrastructure and other important targets. Establishing international norms and agreements that promote responsible behavior in cyberspace, and improving international cooperation and information sharing to detect and prevent cyber attacks, are some of the solutions suggested to improve global cybersecurity.

Quiz (Solutions in Appendix)

1. How can organizations detect and prevent attacks that do not follow the traditional Cyber Kill Chain model?
2. What role can individuals play in preventing cyber attacks that target their personal devices and data?
3. How can organizations ensure that their employees are aware of the threats posed by social engineering attacks, and how can they train them to recognize and avoid these attacks?
4. What can organizations do to prevent cyber attacks from insider threats, such as employees with malicious intent or those who unintentionally compromise security?
5. How can organizations improve incident response and reduce the time to detect and respond to cyber attacks?
6. What role can threat intelligence play in helping organizations identify and prevent cyber attacks before they happen?
7. How can organizations ensure that their security controls are effective and up-to-date, given the constantly evolving

nature of cyber threats?

8. What can organizations do to ensure that their supply chain partners and third-party vendors are not compromising their security?

9. How can organizations prevent data exfiltration and ensure the security of their sensitive data, even in the event of a successful cyber attack?

10. What role can governments and international organizations play in promoting global cybersecurity and preventing cyber attacks on critical infrastructure and other important targets?

3

Hacking Concepts

Hacking generally refers to the act of gaining unauthorized access to a computer system, network, or software application in order to manipulate, steal, or disrupt its contents or operations. The term "hacking" can also refer to the skillful use of computer programming and technical knowledge to overcome limitations in software or hardware systems, or to improve the performance or functionality of such systems.

Hacking can be done for a variety of reasons, including for personal gain, to expose vulnerabilities in a system for the purpose of improving security, or as a means of protest or activism. However, it is important to note that unauthorized hacking is illegal and can have serious consequences, including criminal charges, fines, and imprisonment.

Hacker Types

There are generally three types of hackers based on their intentions and motivations:

1. White hat hackers: Also known as ethical hackers, these are individuals who use their hacking skills for the purpose of identifying and fixing security vulnerabilities in computer systems, networks, and software applications. White hat hackers are usually employed by companies or organizations to test their systems and improve their security measures. They work with the consent and authorization of the system owners.
2. Black hat hackers: These are individuals who use their hacking skills to gain unauthorized access to computer systems, networks, or software applications for personal gain or malicious intent. They may steal or manipulate sensitive data, cause system disruptions or damage, or use the compromised systems for other illegal activities.
3. Grey hat hackers: These are individuals who fall somewhere between the white hat and black hat categories. They may hack into systems without authorization, but their intentions may not be entirely malicious. They may, for example, expose security vulnerabilities to system owners without seeking any financial gain. Grey hat hackers are not authorized to hack into systems, but they may not have malicious intent.

It's important to note that while white hat hacking is legal and even encouraged in some cases, black hat hacking and grey hat hacking are illegal and can result in severe consequences.

White Hat Hacker

White hat hackers are also known as ethical hackers, and they use their hacking skills for the purpose of identifying and fixing security vulnerabilities in computer systems, networks, and software applications. White hat hackers are typically employed by companies or organizations to test their systems and improve their security measures.

Some common activities that white hat hackers engage in include vulnerability assessments, penetration testing, and security audits. They use various tools and techniques to test the security of a system and identify any weaknesses or vulnerabilities that could be exploited by malicious actors.

Once they have identified vulnerabilities, white hat hackers work with the system owners to address and fix the issues. They may also provide recommendations for improving the system's overall security posture.

White hat hacking is generally considered legal and ethical, as long as the hacking is done with the consent and authorization of the system owner. Many organizations rely on white hat hackers to help them stay ahead of potential cyber threats and protect sensitive data.

One real-world example of white hat hackers is the annual Pwn2Own hacking competition, organized by the Zero Day Initiative (ZDI), which is a program run by cybersecurity company Trend Micro. The competition brings together some of the world's top white hat hackers to test their skills against various software and hardware systems.

In the competition, white hat hackers are invited to identify and exploit vulnerabilities in various systems, including web browsers, operating systems, and virtual machines. The competition offers significant cash prizes for successful exploits, and the systems owners are given the opportunity to patch the vulnerabilities before the exploits are made public.

The Pwn2Own competition provides a way for white hat hackers to test their skills against real-world systems, while also helping to identify and fix vulnerabilities in those systems. It also highlights the importance of ethical hacking and the need for organizations to take proactive steps to protect their systems from cyber threats.

Here are some ethical hacking competitions and events that are held annually:

1. Pwn2Own: A hacking competition organized by the Zero Day Initiative (ZDI), which challenges participants to find and exploit vulnerabilities in various software and hardware systems.
2. Global CyberLympics: A global cybersecurity competition that brings together teams of ethical hackers to compete in various challenges related to network defense, digital forensics, and other cybersecurity topics.
3. DEF CON CTF: A hacking competition organized by DEF CON, one of the world's largest hacker conferences. The competition challenges participants to identify and exploit vulnerabilities in a simulated network environment.

4. CyberPatriot: A national high school cybersecurity competition in the United States that challenges teams of students to identify and fix cybersecurity vulnerabilities in simulated network environments.
5. Hack the Pentagon: A program run by the U.S. Department of Defense that invites ethical hackers to test the cybersecurity of select defense systems in exchange for rewards.
6. European Cyber Security Challenge: A European cybersecurity competition that challenges teams of ethical hackers to solve various challenges related to network defense, cryptography, and other cybersecurity topics.

These competitions provide a way for ethical hackers to test their skills against real-world systems and challenges, while also helping to raise awareness about the importance of cybersecurity and the need for organizations to take proactive steps to protect their systems.

Black Hat Hacker

Black hat hackers are individuals who use their hacking skills for malicious purposes, often for personal gain or to cause harm to others. They may use their skills to gain unauthorized access to computer systems, networks, or software applications in order to steal sensitive data, damage or disrupt systems, or carry out other illegal activities.

Black hat hackers use a variety of techniques to carry out their attacks, including social engineering, malware, phishing, and brute force attacks. They may also exploit vulnerabilities in software or hardware systems to gain access.

The activities of black hat hackers are illegal and can have serious consequences, including criminal charges, fines, and imprisonment. They can cause significant financial and reputational damage to individuals and organizations, and their actions can put sensitive data and personal information at risk.

There have been numerous high-profile examples of black hat hackers in recent years. One notable example is the WannaCry ransomware attack, which occurred in May 2017 and affected hundreds of thousands of computers worldwide.

The WannaCry attack was carried out using a vulnerability in Microsoft Windows operating systems that had been previously exploited by the U.S. National Security Agency (NSA). A group of black hat hackers known as the Shadow Brokers obtained the NSA's hacking tools and released them online, which allowed the WannaCry attackers to take advantage of the vulnerability.

The attack involved the use of ransomware, which encrypted the files on infected computers and demanded payment in exchange for a decryption key. The attack affected organizations in more than 150 countries, including the United Kingdom's National Health Service (NHS), which had to cancel thousands of appointments and surgeries as a result.

The WannaCry attack was a clear example of black hat hackers using their skills for malicious purposes, causing significant disruption and financial damage to organizations around the world. It highlights the need for individuals and organizations to take proactive steps to protect their systems from cyber threats and to be aware of the potential consequences of a successful attack.

It's important for individuals and organizations to take steps to protect themselves against black hat hackers, such as implementing strong password policies, using anti-virus and anti-malware software, and regularly updating software and security systems.

Grey Hat Hackers

Grey hat hackers are individuals who, like black hat hackers, use their hacking skills to gain unauthorized access to computer systems, networks, or software applications. However, unlike black hat hackers, their intentions may not be entirely malicious. They may hack into systems without authorization, but they may do so in order to expose security vulnerabilities or flaws in the system.

Grey hat hackers may use their skills to identify weaknesses in a system, and then attempt to alert the system owner or administrator to those weaknesses in order to encourage them to take action to address the issue. They may do this without seeking financial gain or causing damage to the system.

However, while grey hat hackers may have good intentions, their actions are still illegal and can carry significant consequences. They are not authorized to hack into systems, and even if they do so with the intention of helping, they can still be subject to criminal charges and other penalties.

It's important to note that there are legal and ethical ways to report security vulnerabilities or flaws in a system, and individuals who want to help improve system security should follow established procedures for doing so rather than resorting to unauthorized hacking.

Grey hat hacking is a controversial area, and it can be difficult to identify specific examples of individuals who have engaged in grey hat hacking without crossing into the realm of black hat hacking.

One example of grey hat hacking is the case of Marcus Hutchins, a cybersecurity researcher who was credited with stopping the WannaCry ransomware attack. Hutchins was later arrested and charged with creating and distributing malware known as Kronos, which was used to steal banking credentials.

While Hutchins did not use the Kronos malware himself, he did create a version of it that was used by others. However, he also made efforts to disrupt the spread of the malware and prevent it from being used for malicious purposes.

The case of Marcus Hutchins is an example of grey hat hacking because he was both involved in the creation of a piece of malware and also made efforts to mitigate its effects. The legal proceedings surrounding his case are complex and contro-versial, and highlight the difficult ethical and legal questions surrounding grey hat hacking.

Hacking Tools and Techniques

Hackers use a variety of tools and techniques to carry out their attacks, including:

1. Social engineering: This involves using psychological manipulation to trick individuals into divulging sensitive information or performing actions that they wouldn't normally do. Common tactics include pretexting, baiting, and phishing.
2. Phishing: Phishing is a type of social engineering attack that involves creating a fake website or email that appears to be from a legitimate source, in order to trick individuals into entering their sensitive information such as login credentials, credit card numbers or other personal information.
3. Malware: Malware is a type of software designed to gain unauthorized access to a computer system or network. Common types of malware include viruses, Trojans, and ransomware.
4. Brute force attacks: A brute force attack involves trying every possible combination of characters to guess a password or other piece of sensitive information. This technique can be time-consuming but can be effective against weak passwords.
5. SQL injection: SQL injection is a technique used to exploit vulnerabilities in web applications. By injecting SQL commands into web application input fields, hackers can gain access to sensitive data stored in the application's database.
6. Denial of Service (DoS) attacks: A DoS attack involves

flooding a network or website with traffic in order to overwhelm its servers and prevent legitimate users from accessing the service.

These are just a few of the many tools and techniques used by hackers to carry out their attacks. As the cybersecurity landscape continues to evolve, new techniques and tools are constantly being developed, highlighting the importance of staying up-to-date with the latest trends and best practices in cybersecurity.

Social Engineering

Social engineering is a technique used by hackers to manipulate individuals into divulging sensitive information or performing actions that they wouldn't normally do. Social engineering attacks typically involve psychological manipulation, rather than technical exploits or software vulnerabilities.

Examples of social engineering attacks include:

1. Phishing: This involves sending fake emails that appear to be from a legitimate source, such as a bank or online retailer, in order to trick individuals into entering their login credentials or other sensitive information on a fake website.
2. Pretexting: This involves creating a false scenario or pretext in order to gain the trust of the individual and extract sensitive information. For example, a hacker might pretend to be a customer service representative and ask for account information in order to "verify" the customer's

identity.

3. Baiting: This involves enticing individuals with a free or valuable offer, such as a USB drive or gift card, in order to get them to divulge sensitive information or perform an action that could compromise their security.

4. Scareware: This involves using scare tactics, such as fake warnings about viruses or malware, in order to convince individuals to download and install malicious software on their computers.

Social engineering attacks can be difficult to detect, as they often rely on human psychology rather than technical vulnerabilities. The best defense against social engineering attacks is to stay vigilant and be aware of the potential risks, and to follow best practices for online security, such as using strong passwords and being cautious when clicking on links or downloading attachments from unknown sources.

Phishing

Phishing is a type of social engineering attack that involves sending fake emails or messages to individuals in order to trick them into revealing sensitive information or performing an action that could compromise their security. Phishing attacks typically involve impersonating a legitimate source, such as a bank, online retailer, or government agency, in order to gain the trust of the individual and extract sensitive information.

Phishing attacks can take many forms, including:

1. Email phishing: This involves sending fake emails that

appear to be from a legitimate source, such as a bank or online retailer, in order to trick individuals into entering their login credentials or other sensitive information on a fake website.

2. Smishing: This involves sending fake text messages that appear to be from a legitimate source, in order to trick individuals into revealing sensitive information or clicking on a malicious link.

3. Spear phishing: This is a targeted phishing attack that is customized for a specific individual or organization. The attacker may gather information about the target from social media or other sources in order to create a more convincing phishing email.

4. Whaling: This is a type of spear phishing attack that targets high-level executives or other individuals with access to sensitive information.

Phishing attacks can be difficult to detect, as they often rely on social engineering techniques and may appear to be from a legitimate source. The best defense against phishing attacks is to stay vigilant and be aware of the potential risks, and to follow best practices for online security, such as using strong passwords, being cautious when clicking on links or downloading attachments from unknown sources, and regularly updating software and security systems.

Malware

Malware, short for "malicious software," is a type of software designed to gain unauthorized access to a computer system or network, cause damage or disruption to the system, or steal sensitive information. Malware can take many forms, including viruses, Trojans, and ransomware.

Examples of malware include:

1. Viruses: These are programs that infect other programs or files on a computer and spread from one computer to another. Viruses can be designed to delete files, steal sensitive information, or cause other types of damage to the system.
2. Trojans: These are programs that disguise themselves as legitimate software in order to trick individuals into downloading and installing them. Trojans can be designed to steal sensitive information or give hackers remote access to the infected system.
3. Ransomware: This is a type of malware that encrypts the files on an infected system and demands payment in exchange for a decryption key. Ransomware can be difficult to remove and can cause significant financial and reputational damage to individuals and organizations.
4. Adware: This is software that displays unwanted advertisements or pop-ups on a user's computer. While not typically as harmful as other types of malware, adware can be annoying and may slow down the system.

Malware can be distributed through a variety of channels, including email attachments, malicious websites, or infected software downloads. To protect against malware, individuals and organizations should use anti-virus and anti-malware software, keep software and security systems up-to-date, and be cautious when clicking on links or downloading attachments from unknown sources.

Brute force attacks

A brute force attack is a technique used by hackers to crack a password or other security mechanism by trying every possible combination of characters until the correct one is found. Brute force attacks are often used against weak passwords or encryption keys, and can be time-consuming but can be effective in some cases.

Brute force attacks can take many forms, including:

1. Password guessing: This involves trying commonly used passwords or other combinations of characters in order to guess the correct password for a user's account.
2. Dictionary attacks: This involves using a pre-defined list of words or phrases in order to guess the correct password. Dictionary attacks can be more effective than password guessing because they are based on real words and phrases that are more likely to be used as passwords.
3. Rainbow table attacks: This involves using pre-computed tables of password hashes in order to quickly find the corresponding plaintext passwords. Rainbow table attacks can be more efficient than other types of brute force attacks, but require significant computing power and storage resources.

To protect against brute force attacks, individuals and organizations should use strong passwords that are difficult to guess or crack, and use two-factor authentication or other security measures to provide an additional layer of protection. Additionally, software and security systems should be regularly updated to address vulnerabilities that could be exploited by brute force attacks.

SQL injection

SQL injection is a technique used by hackers to exploit vulnerabilities in web applications that use SQL databases. SQL injection attacks involve inserting malicious SQL code into input fields on a website, such as login forms or search boxes, in order to gain unauthorized access to sensitive data stored in the database.

SQL injection attacks can take many forms, including:

1. Authentication bypass: This involves inserting malicious code into the login form of a web application in order to bypass authentication and gain access to the system.
2. Data theft: This involves inserting malicious code into the search box or other input fields of a web application in order to retrieve sensitive data from the database.
3. Denial of Service (DoS) attacks: This involves using SQL injection attacks to overload the database with requests, causing the website to slow down or crash.

To protect against SQL injection attacks, web application developers should follow best practices for secure coding, such as using parameterized queries and input validation to prevent malicious code from being injected into the database. Additionally, web application owners should regularly scan their websites for vulnerabilities and implement security measures to protect against SQL injection attacks, such as using web application firewalls or intrusion detection systems.

Denial of Service (DoS) attacks

A Denial of Service (DoS) attack is a type of cyberattack that aims to disrupt the normal functioning of a computer system or network, making it unavailable to users. DoS attacks typically involve flooding a targeted system or network with traffic, overwhelming its resources and causing it to become unresponsive or crash.

DoS attacks can take many forms, including:

1. Network-based attacks: This involves flooding a network with traffic, such as through Distributed Denial of Service (DDoS) attacks, in which multiple computers are used to generate traffic and overwhelm the target.
2. Application-based attacks: This involves overwhelming a specific application, such as a website or email server, with traffic in order to make it unavailable to users.
3. Protocol-based attacks: This involves exploiting vulnerabilities in network protocols, such as TCP/IP, to disrupt network communications and cause systems to become unresponsive.

DoS attacks can be costly and damaging to individuals and organizations, as they can disrupt normal business operations and cause significant financial losses. To protect against DoS attacks, individuals and organizations should implement security measures such as firewalls, intrusion detection systems, and DoS mitigation services. Additionally, it is important to regularly update software and security systems to address vulnerabilities that could be exploited by DoS attacks.

Discussion

Organizations can balance accessibility and security by implementing multi-factor authentication, regularly updating software and security systems, and providing regular security training to employees. This can ensure that access is controlled and protected, while still allowing legitimate users to access the system.

White hat hackers should follow responsible disclosure practices when identifying and disclosing vulnerabilities in systems. This includes working with system owners to patch vulnerabilities before making them public, and respecting the privacy and security of the system and its users.

Individuals can protect themselves from phishing attacks and other forms of social engineering by being cautious when clicking on links or downloading attachments from unknown sources, using strong passwords, and being aware of the potential risks of sharing sensitive information online.

Software developers can create more secure applications and systems by using secure coding practices, such as input validation and parameterized queries, and regularly testing their applications for vulnerabilities.

Law enforcement and government agencies can effectively

combat cybercrime and hacking by working with international partners, implementing strong cybersecurity policies, and providing education and resources to the public.

Successful hacking attempts on critical infrastructure systems, such as power grids or transportation networks, can have severe consequences, including power outages, transportation disruptions, and financial losses. To mitigate these risks, organizations should implement strong security measures, such as firewalls and intrusion detection systems, and conduct regular security audits and vulnerability assessments.

Individuals and organizations can protect themselves against ransomware attacks by using anti-virus and anti-malware software, regularly updating software and security systems, and backing up important data regularly.

The proliferation of IoT has created new vulnerabilities and attack vectors. To mitigate the risks, organizations and individuals should implement strong security measures, such as network segmentation and strong authentication protocols.

Individuals and organizations can protect their sensitive data from being stolen by hackers by using strong passwords, encryption, and two-factor authentication to protect their sensitive data from being stolen by hackers.

Public-private partnerships can improve overall cybersecurity and reduce the risk of hacking attempts by involving information sharing, joint exercises and training, and collaboration on cybersecurity policy and regulation.

Quiz (Solutions in Appendix)

1. How can organizations strike a balance between providing accessibility to their systems while also securing them against hacking attempts?
2. What ethical considerations should white hat hackers take into account when identifying and disclosing vulnerabilities in systems?
3. How can individuals protect themselves from phishing attacks and other forms of social engineering?
4. How can software developers create more secure applications and systems?
5. How can law enforcement and government agencies effectively combat cybercrime and hacking?
6. What are the potential consequences of a successful hacking attempt on critical infrastructure systems, such as power grids or transportation networks?
7. How can individuals and organizations protect themselves against ransomware attacks?
8. What impact has the proliferation of the Internet of Things (IoT) had on cybersecurity, and what steps can be taken to mitigate the risks?
9. How can individuals and organizations protect their sensitive data from being stolen by hackers?
10. How can the public and private sectors work together to improve overall cybersecurity and reduce the risk of hacking attempts?

4

Ethical Hacking Concepts

Ethical hacking refers to the process of identifying and exploiting vulnerabilities in computer systems and networks with the goal of improving their security. Ethical hacking is carried out by trained professionals who have been given permission to test the security of a system, and its main objective is to identify and fix potential security issues before malicious attackers can exploit them.

Ethical hacking is a critical process in today's world because it helps organizations to secure their systems and networks against cyberattacks. By identifying vulnerabilities and weaknesses, ethical hackers help organizations to improve their overall security posture and prevent data breaches, financial loss, and reputational damage.

Ethical hacking involves a wide range of techniques and methodologies, including network scanning, port scanning, vulnerability scanning, social engineering, and penetration testing. These techniques are used to identify weaknesses in a system, such as software vulnerabilities, misconfigurations, weak passwords, and other security issues.

Ethical hacking is different from malicious hacking because it is carried out with the permission of the system owner and is intended to improve the security of the system rather than cause harm. Ethical hackers adhere to a strict code of ethics that includes obtaining permission before testing a system, protecting confidential information, and reporting any vulnerabilities discovered to the system owner.

The role of ethical hackers in information security is crucial, as they play a vital role in identifying potential vulnerabilities and weaknesses in computer systems and networks before malicious hackers can exploit them. Ethical hackers use their skills and knowledge to test and evaluate the security of a system and report any weaknesses and vulnerabilities to the system owner, so they can be fixed before they can be exploited by attackers.

Ethical hackers use a range of techniques and methodologies, including network scanning, vulnerability scanning, penetration testing, and social engineering to identify potential weaknesses and vulnerabilities in a system. They analyze the results of these tests and provide detailed reports to system owners about any security flaws they have identified, along with recommendations for remediation.

One of the primary roles of ethical hackers is to perform penetration testing, which involves attempting to exploit vulnerabilities in a system in order to determine its resilience to attack. By conducting a simulated attack, ethical hackers can identify areas of weakness and provide recommendations for improving the security of the system.

Ethical hackers also play a critical role in educating organizations about the importance of security and best practices for maintaining secure systems and networks. They can provide training and guidance to staff on how to avoid falling prey to social engineering attacks, how to create strong passwords, and how to keep software up-to-date to prevent known vulnerabilities from being exploited.

In summary, the role of ethical hackers in information security is vital to ensuring the safety and security of computer systems and networks. They use their skills and knowledge to identify potential vulnerabilities and weaknesses, perform penetration testing, and provide recommendations for improving the security of the system. Ethical hackers also play a role in educating organizations about the importance of security and best practices for maintaining secure systems and networks.

Ethical Hacking Process

The process of ethical hacking involves several steps that are essential to identify potential vulnerabilities and weaknesses in a computer system or network. The following are the typical steps involved in ethical hacking:

1. Reconnaissance: This involves gathering information about the target system or network. This information could include the target's IP address, operating system, open ports, and services running on the system. The

information is collected using both passive and active techniques, such as social engineering, DNS queries, and port scanning.

2. Scanning: In this step, the ethical hacker uses tools to identify vulnerabilities and weaknesses in the target system or network. This could include port scanning, vulnerability scanning, and network mapping.

3. Enumeration: This involves gathering more detailed information about the target system or network, such as user accounts, password policies, and network shares. This information is critical to identifying potential vulnerabilities that can be exploited.

4. Vulnerability analysis: The ethical hacker analyzes the information collected in the previous steps to identify vulnerabilities that can be exploited. This includes analyzing the results of vulnerability scans, reviewing system configurations, and analyzing network traffic.

5. Exploitation: Once vulnerabilities have been identified, the ethical hacker attempts to exploit them to gain access to the target system or network. This can include running exploits, using social engineering techniques, or attempting to gain access to system passwords.

6. Post-exploitation: After gaining access to the target system or network, the ethical hacker will perform additional tasks such as privilege escalation, data exfiltration, or planting backdoors. This step is essential to determine the impact of the successful exploitation and to ensure that all vulnerabilities are remediated.

7. Reporting: After the ethical hacker has completed the testing, a comprehensive report is prepared outlining the vulnerabilities and weaknesses that were identified, the

methods used to exploit them, and recommendations for remediation.

Reconnaissance: Step 1

Reconnaissance is the first step in the process of ethical hacking. It is the process of gathering information about the target system or network that is to be tested. The information gathered during this phase is used to identify potential vulnerabilities that can be exploited in later stages of the ethical hacking process.

Reconnaissance can be divided into two categories: active and passive reconnaissance. Active reconnaissance involves direct interaction with the target system or network, while passive reconnaissance involves collecting information without direct interaction.

Active reconnaissance techniques include scanning the target system or network, probing the network for open ports and services, and performing network traffic analysis. This information is used to identify the operating system and software versions running on the target system, which can be used to identify potential vulnerabilities.

Passive reconnaissance techniques include gathering information from public sources such as the target organization's website, social media profiles, and online forums. This information can be used to identify potential employees, email addresses, and other sensitive information that can be used in social engineering attacks.

The reconnaissance phase is critical because it provides essential information about the target system or network. Without accurate and complete information, the ethical hacker may miss potential vulnerabilities, leading to an incomplete testing process.

However, it is important to note that while reconnaissance is a necessary step in the ethical hacking process, it should be carried out within legal and ethical boundaries. Ethical hackers must obtain permission from the system or network owner before performing any testing and must adhere to the terms of the testing agreement to ensure that the testing process is carried out within acceptable boundaries.

Scanning: Step 2

Scanning is the second step in the ethical hacking process, following reconnaissance. It is the process of identifying active hosts, open ports, and services running on the target system or network. The purpose of scanning is to determine the network topology and identify potential vulnerabilities that can be exploited.

There are different types of scans that can be performed during this phase, including port scanning, vulnerability scanning, and network mapping. Port scanning involves scanning the target system or network to identify open ports and the services running on them. Vulnerability scanning involves identifying potential vulnerabilities in the target system or network. Network mapping involves identifying the topology of the target network.

47

Scanning can be performed using both automated tools and manual techniques. Automated tools are often used to perform initial scans and provide quick results. However, manual techniques can provide more detailed information and can help identify more complex vulnerabilities.

The results of the scanning phase are used to identify potential vulnerabilities in the target system or network. This information is then used to plan the next steps of the ethical hacking process, such as enumeration and vulnerability analysis.

It is important to note that while scanning is a necessary step in the ethical hacking process, it should be carried out within legal and ethical boundaries. Ethical hackers must obtain permission from the system or network owner before performing any testing and must adhere to the terms of the testing agreement to ensure that the testing process is carried out within acceptable boundaries. Additionally, the scanning process must be conducted carefully to avoid disrupting the target system or network.

Enumeration: Step 3

Enumeration is the third step in the ethical hacking process, following reconnaissance and scanning. It is the process of actively probing the target system or network to gather more detailed information about its resources and users. The purpose of enumeration is to identify potential vulnerabilities that can be exploited and to gain a better understanding of the target system or network.

Enumeration involves using different techniques to gather information about the target system or network, such as user account names, system settings, installed applications, network shares, and other resources. The techniques used in enumeration can include banner grabbing, SNMP (Simple Network Management Protocol) enumeration, and LDAP (Lightweight Directory Access Protocol) enumeration, among others.

One of the main goals of enumeration is to identify user account names and passwords. This information can be used to attempt to gain unauthorized access to the target system or network. Enumeration can also be used to identify other potential vulnerabilities, such as outdated software versions, misconfigured systems, and open network shares.

Enumeration can be performed using automated tools or manual techniques. Automated tools can provide quick results and identify potential vulnerabilities, but manual techniques can provide more detailed information about the target system or network.

It is important to note that while enumeration is a necessary step in the ethical hacking process, it should be carried out within legal and ethical boundaries. Ethical hackers must obtain permission from the system or network owner before performing any testing and must adhere to the terms of the testing agreement to ensure that the testing process is carried out within acceptable boundaries. Additionally, the enumeration process must be conducted carefully to avoid disrupting the target system or network.

Vulnerability analysis: Step 4

Vulnerability analysis is the fourth step in the ethical hacking process, following reconnaissance, scanning, and enumeration. It is the process of analyzing the information collected during the previous phases to identify potential vulnerabilities that can be exploited. The purpose of vulnerability analysis is to determine which vulnerabilities are exploitable and to identify the potential impact of an exploit.

Vulnerability analysis involves using different techniques to analyze the information collected during the reconnaissance, scanning, and enumeration phases. This can include reviewing system configurations, analyzing network traffic, and analyzing the results of vulnerability scans.

The vulnerability analysis phase can be broken down into two main parts: identifying potential vulnerabilities and assessing the severity of those vulnerabilities. The identification process involves reviewing the results of the previous phases to identify potential vulnerabilities, such as outdated software versions, misconfigured systems, and weak passwords. The severity assessment involves determining the potential impact of a vulnerability if it were to be exploited.

The results of the vulnerability analysis phase are used to determine which vulnerabilities should be prioritized for exploitation. This information is used to plan the next steps of the ethical hacking process, such as exploitation and post-exploitation.

It is important to note that while vulnerability analysis is a necessary step in the ethical hacking process, it should be carried out within legal and ethical boundaries. Ethical hackers must obtain permission from the system or network owner before performing any testing and must adhere to the terms of the testing agreement to ensure that the testing process is carried out within acceptable boundaries. Additionally, the vulnerability analysis process must be conducted carefully to avoid disrupting the target system or network.

Exploitation: Step 5

Exploitation is the fifth step in the ethical hacking process, following reconnaissance, scanning, enumeration, and vulnerability analysis. It is the process of attempting to exploit the identified vulnerabilities in the target system or network to gain unauthorized access or to perform other malicious activities.

Exploitation involves using different techniques to attempt to exploit the identified vulnerabilities. This can include running exploits, using social engineering techniques, or attempting to gain access to system passwords. The goal of exploitation is to gain access to the target system or network and to gather sensitive information or perform other malicious activities.

Before attempting exploitation, ethical hackers must verify that the identified vulnerabilities are exploitable and that they are not causing any harm to the target system or network. This is important to ensure that the ethical hacking process is carried out within acceptable boundaries and does not cause any damage to the target system or network.

It is also important to note that exploitation should only be performed after obtaining permission from the system or network owner and adhering to the terms of the testing agreement. The ethical hacker should ensure that any information obtained during the exploitation phase is kept confidential and is only shared with the system or network owner.

The results of the exploitation phase are used to demonstrate the potential impact of the identified vulnerabilities and to provide recommendations for remediation. This information is used to plan the next steps of the ethical hacking process, such as post-exploitation and reporting.

In summary, exploitation is a critical step in the ethical hacking process, as it involves attempting to exploit the identified vulnerabilities in the target system or network. Ethical hackers must verify that the vulnerabilities are exploitable and must obtain permission from the system or network owner before attempting exploitation. The results of the exploitation phase are used to demonstrate the potential impact of the identified vulnerabilities and to provide recommendations for remediation.

Post-exploitation: Step 6

Post-exploitation is the sixth step in the ethical hacking process, following reconnaissance, scanning, enumeration, vulnerability analysis, and exploitation. It is the process of performing additional tasks after gaining unauthorized access to the target system or network to maintain access, gather additional information, or perform other malicious activities.

Post-exploitation involves using different techniques to maintain access to the target system or network. This can include planting backdoors, creating new user accounts, or modifying existing user accounts. The goal of post-exploitation is to ensure that the ethical hacker can continue to access the target system or network even if the initial method of exploitation is detected and remediated.

Ethical hackers may also use post-exploitation techniques to gather additional information about the target system or network. This information can be used to identify additional vulnerabilities that can be exploited in future testing or to gather sensitive information that can be used in social engineering attacks.

It is important to note that post-exploitation should only be performed after obtaining permission from the system or network owner and adhering to the terms of the testing agreement. The ethical hacker should ensure that any information obtained during the post-exploitation phase is kept confidential and is only shared with the system or network owner.

The results of the post-exploitation phase are used to provide a comprehensive report to the system or network owner that outlines the potential impact of the identified vulnerabilities and provides recommendations for remediation. This information is used to improve the security of the target system or network and to prevent future unauthorized access or malicious activities.

In summary, post-exploitation is a critical step in the ethical hacking process, as it involves performing additional tasks after gaining unauthorized access to the target system or network to maintain access, gather additional information, or perform other malicious activities. Ethical hackers must obtain permission from the system or network owner before performing any testing and must adhere to the terms of the testing agreement to ensure that the testing process is carried out within acceptable boundaries.

Reporting: Step 7

Reporting is the final step in the ethical hacking process, following reconnaissance, scanning, enumeration, vulnerability analysis, exploitation, and post-exploitation. It is the process of creating a comprehensive report that outlines the potential vulnerabilities and weaknesses identified during the testing process and provides recommendations for remediation.

The report is an essential deliverable in the ethical hacking process, as it provides a summary of the testing process and the potential impact of the identified vulnerabilities on the target system or network. The report should include a detailed explanation of the testing methodology used, the vulnerabilities identified, the potential impact of those vulnerabilities, and recommendations for remediation.

The report should also include any supporting documentation, such as screenshots, network diagrams, and system configurations, to provide a clear and detailed explanation of the testing process and the vulnerabilities identified.

It is important to note that the report should be written in a clear and concise manner, with technical terms explained in plain language. The report should also adhere to any legal or regulatory requirements that apply to the organization being tested.

The report should be presented to the system or network owner, along with a debriefing session to review the findings and recommendations. The debriefing session should provide an opportunity for the ethical hacker to explain the vulnerabilities identified and the potential impact of those vulnerabilities on the organization. It should also provide an opportunity for the system or network owner to ask questions and provide feedback.

Discussion

Ethical hacking is a critical process that helps organizations identify potential vulnerabilities in their systems and networks. It is essential to consider ethical considerations, legal require-ments, and potential challenges when performing an ethical hacking test.

When conducting an ethical hacking test, ethical hackers must obtain permission from the system or network owner and adhere to the terms of the testing agreement. It is crucial to ensure that the testing process does not cause any harm to the target system or network.

During the testing process, ethical hackers commonly identify vulnerabilities such as outdated software versions, weak pass-words, misconfigured systems, and open network shares. By identifying these vulnerabilities, ethical hackers can provide recommendations for remediation to improve the security posture of the target system or network.

Ethical hacking can help organizations improve their cybersecurity posture by identifying potential vulnerabilities and weaknesses in their systems and networks. Organizations can use the results of an ethical hacking test to develop a plan for remediation, which can improve their overall security posture.

Social engineering techniques can be used to obtain sensitive information from individuals, which could violate their privacy. Ethical hackers must ensure that these techniques are used within acceptable ethical boundaries and must obtain permission from the system or network owner before using them.

Ethical hacking differs from malicious hacking in that it is performed with the permission of the system or network owner and is focused on identifying vulnerabilities for the purpose of improving security. Malicious hacking is performed without permission and is focused on causing harm to the target system or network.

Ethical hackers must ensure that the testing process does not violate any laws or regulations and must obtain the necessary permissions and waivers before performing any testing. By adhering to legal considerations, ethical hackers can ensure that their testing process is conducted within acceptable boundaries.

Ethical hackers can keep their skills up-to-date and stay informed about new threats and vulnerabilities by attending training courses, conferences, and webinars, and participating in online communities.

During the testing process, ethical hackers may face challenges such as unresponsive system owners, limited access to resources, and new and emerging threats and vulnerabilities. By overcoming these challenges, ethical hackers can ensure that their testing process is conducted within acceptable boundaries.

Organizations can use the results of an ethical hacking test to identify potential vulnerabilities and weaknesses in their systems and networks and develop a plan for remediation to improve their overall security posture. By taking action to address identified vulnerabilities, organizations can improve their security posture and reduce the risk of a security breach.

Quiz (Solutions in Appendix)

1. What are some ethical considerations that ethical hackers must take into account when performing a penetration test?
2. What are some of the most common vulnerabilities that ethical hackers identify during the testing process?
3. How can ethical hacking help organizations to improve their cybersecurity posture?
4. What are some of the ethical implications of using social engineering techniques during an ethical hacking test?
5. How does ethical hacking differ from malicious hacking?
6. What are some of the legal considerations that ethical hackers must take into account during the testing process?
7. How do ethical hackers keep their skills up-to-date and

stay informed about new threats and vulnerabilities?
8. How can ethical hacking be used to test the security of cloud-based systems and applications?
9. What are some of the challenges that ethical hackers may face during the testing process?
10. How can organizations use the results of an ethical hacking test to improve their overall security posture?

5

Information Security Controls

Information security controls can be categorized into three main types: administrative, physical, and technical. Each type of control serves a distinct purpose in securing an organization's information assets.

Administrative Controls:

Administrative controls are policies, procedures, and guidelines that are established by an organization to manage the behavior and actions of its employees, contractors, and partners. Some examples of administrative controls include:

- Security policies and procedures
- Risk assessments and audits
- Security awareness training for employees
- Access control policies and procedures
- Incident response and disaster recovery planning
- Security compliance monitoring and enforcement

Physical Controls:

Physical controls are measures designed to protect an organization's information assets by restricting access to the physical spaces where those assets are stored. Some examples of physical controls include:

- Security guards and surveillance cameras
- Access control systems, such as key cards and biometric scanners
- Locks and barriers
- Environmental controls, such as fire suppression systems and temperature control
- Secure storage areas for sensitive data

Technical Controls:

Technical controls are tools and technologies that are used to protect an organization's information assets from unauthorized access, alteration, or destruction. Some examples of technical controls include:

- Firewalls, intrusion detection and prevention systems (IDS/IPS)
- Encryption technologies, such as SSL/TLS, PGP, and S/MIME
- Antivirus and anti-malware software
- Network security protocols, such as VPNs and VLANs
- Access control technologies, such as multi-factor authentication and biometric authentication

It's important for organizations to implement a combination of administrative, physical, and technical controls to ensure comprehensive information security. Each type of control has its own strengths and weaknesses, and by using a layered approach, organizations can create a strong defense against a variety of threats.

Information Security Controls

There are various types of information security controls that can be implemented to protect an organization's information assets. Here are some examples of commonly used controls:

Access Control:

Access control is a security measure that restricts access to resources based on the identity of the user or device. Examples of access control include:

- Passwords and passphrases
- Biometric authentication, such as fingerprint scanning and facial recognition
- Multi-factor authentication, such as requiring a password and a security token or smart card

Encryption:

Encryption is the process of converting information into a code or cipher so that it can only be read by authorized parties. Examples of encryption include:

- SSL/TLS, which encrypts data in transit between web browsers and servers
- Disk encryption, which encrypts data on storage devices such as hard drives and flash drives
- Email encryption, such as PGP and S/MIME, which encrypts email messages to protect their contents from unauthorized access

Firewalls:

Firewalls are network security devices that control access to a network by filtering incoming and outgoing traffic. Examples of firewalls include:

- Network firewalls, which filter traffic between a private network and the internet
- Host-based firewalls, which filter traffic between a computer and the network it is connected to

Intrusion Detection and Prevention Systems (IDS/IPS):

IDS/IPS are security measures that monitor network traffic for signs of suspicious activity and can either alert security personnel or automatically block the traffic. Examples of IDS/IPS include:

- Network-based IDS/IPS, which analyze network traffic in real-time to detect anomalies
- Host-based IDS/IPS, which monitor a single computer or device for signs of malicious activity

Backup and Recovery:

Backup and recovery measures are used to protect against data loss due to hardware failure, human error, or cyber attacks. Examples of backup and recovery measures include:

- Regularly backing up data to secure locations, such as cloud storage or offline backups
- Testing the backup and recovery process regularly to ensure its effectiveness
- Implementing disaster recovery plans that include procedures for restoring critical systems and data in the event of a disaster

These are just a few examples of information security controls that organizations can implement to protect their information assets. It's important for organizations to assess their risks and select the appropriate controls to mitigate those risks.

Best Practice

Implementing information security controls can be a complex process, but here are some best practices to consider:

1. Conduct a Risk Assessment:
2. Before implementing any security controls, it's important to conduct a thorough risk assessment to identify potential threats and vulnerabilities to your organization's information assets. This assessment will help you determine which security controls are necessary and which areas of your infrastructure require the most attention.

63

3. Develop Security Policies and Procedures:
4. Establishing clear security policies and procedures is crucial for ensuring that everyone in the organization understands their roles and responsibilities when it comes to protecting sensitive data. These policies and procedures should cover topics such as access control, data classification, incident response, and disaster recovery.
5. Implement a Layered Defense:
6. A layered defense strategy involves using multiple security controls to protect your organization's assets. This includes implementing a combination of administrative, physical, and technical controls to ensure comprehensive protection against a variety of threats.
7. Regularly Monitor and Test Your Security Controls:
8. Security controls should be regularly monitored and tested to ensure their effectiveness. This includes performing regular vulnerability scans and penetration tests to identify weaknesses in your infrastructure and address them promptly.
9. Provide Security Awareness Training:
10. All employees, contractors, and partners should be trained on security best practices and the importance of protecting sensitive information. This includes training on how to recognize phishing scams, how to create strong passwords, and how to report security incidents.
11. Stay Up-to-Date on Security Threats and Trends:
12. Keeping up-to-date on the latest security threats and trends is crucial for maintaining an effective security posture. This includes staying informed about the latest vulnerabilities and attacks, as well as attending security conferences and training sessions to learn about new

security technologies and best practices.

By following these best practices, organizations can implement effective information security controls and reduce the risk of a data breach or cyber attack.

Risk Assessment

A risk assessment is a systematic process of identifying, analyzing, and evaluating potential risks that could impact an organization's information assets. Here are some steps to follow when conducting a risk assessment:

1. Identify Information Assets:
2. Start by identifying all the information assets that need to be protected. This includes data, hardware, software, and applications.
3. Identify Threats:
4. Next, identify all the potential threats that could impact those information assets. This includes natural disasters, cyber attacks, human errors, and malicious insiders.
5. Assess Vulnerabilities:
6. Once the threats have been identified, assess the vulnerabilities of your information assets. This includes identifying weaknesses in your infrastructure, such as outdated software, weak passwords, and unsecured network connections.
7. Analyze the Likelihood and Impact:
8. Analyze the likelihood of each potential threat occurring and the impact it could have on your organization. This includes assessing the financial, operational, and reputa-

tional damage that could result from a security incident.

9. Prioritize Risks:

10. Based on the likelihood and impact analysis, prioritize the risks and determine which ones require immediate attention. This will help you develop a plan for addressing the most critical risks first.

11. Develop a Risk Management Plan:

12. Develop a risk management plan that outlines the actions that need to be taken to mitigate the identified risks. This includes implementing security controls, such as access control, encryption, and firewalls, and establishing incident response and disaster recovery plans.

13. Review and Update:

14. Finally, it's important to regularly review and update your risk assessment to ensure that your security controls remain effective and relevant to your organization's changing needs.

By conducting a thorough risk assessment, organizations can identify potential risks and vulnerabilities and develop an effective plan for mitigating them. This can help reduce the risk of a security incident and protect your organization's information assets.

Develop Security Policies and Procedures

Developing clear and comprehensive security policies and procedures is crucial for ensuring that everyone in the organization understands their roles and responsibilities when it comes to protecting sensitive data. Here are some steps to follow when developing security policies and procedures:

1. Establish a Security Policy Framework:
2. Develop a security policy framework that outlines the scope, objectives, and principles of your organization's security program. This framework should be aligned with industry standards and best practices, such as ISO 27001 or NIST Cybersecurity Framework.
3. Identify and Classify Data:
4. Identify all the types of data that your organization handles, and classify them according to their sensitivity and criticality. This will help you determine which data requires the most protection and which security controls are necessary to protect it.
5. Develop Security Policies:
6. Based on the data classification, develop policies that outline the rules and procedures for handling sensitive information. This includes policies for access control, data retention, data backup, and incident response.
7. Establish Standards and Procedures:
8. Develop detailed standards and procedures that support the security policies. This includes procedures for creating and managing user accounts, performing backups, and responding to security incidents.
9. Define Roles and Responsibilities:
10. Clearly define the roles and responsibilities of everyone in the organization when it comes to information security. This includes management, employees, contractors, and partners. Make sure that everyone understands their responsibilities and the consequences of failing to adhere to the security policies and procedures.
11. Communicate and Train:
12. Communicate the security policies and procedures to ev-

eryone in the organization, and provide training to ensure that everyone understands them. This includes new employee orientation, regular security awareness training, and ongoing communication of updates and changes to the policies and procedures.

13. Review and Update:
14. Regularly review and update the security policies and procedures to ensure that they remain effective and relevant to your organization's changing needs. This includes reviewing them after security incidents, changes to the regulatory environment, and major changes to your organization's infrastructure.

By developing clear and comprehensive security policies and procedures, organizations can establish a strong security culture and reduce the risk of a security incident.

Implement a Layered Defense

A layered defense is a security strategy that involves implementing multiple security controls to protect an organization's information assets. Here are some steps to follow when implementing a layered defense:

1. Conduct a Risk Assessment:
2. Start by conducting a risk assessment to identify potential threats and vulnerabilities to your organization's information assets. This will help you determine which security controls are necessary to mitigate the identified risks.
3. Implement Administrative Controls:
4. Implement administrative controls, such as policies, pro-

cedures, and guidelines, to manage the behavior and actions of employees, contractors, and partners. This includes access control policies, incident response and disaster recovery plans, and security awareness training.

5. Implement Physical Controls:

6. Implement physical controls to restrict access to the phys-ical spaces where your organization's information assets are stored. This includes access control systems, such as key cards and biometric scanners, security guards and surveillance cameras, and secure storage areas for sensitive data.

7. Implement Technical Controls:

8. Implement technical controls, such as firewalls, intrusion detection and prevention systems (IDS/IPS), encryption technologies, and access control technologies, to protect your organization's information assets from unauthorized access, alteration, or destruction.

9. Implement Redundancy and Backup Measures:

10. Implement redundancy and backup measures to ensure that your organization's information assets are available and recoverable in the event of a security incident. This includes implementing disaster recovery plans, regularly backing up critical data, and testing the backup and recov-ery process.

11. Regularly Monitor and Test Security Controls:

12. Regularly monitor and test your organization's security controls to ensure their effectiveness. This includes per-forming regular vulnerability scans and penetration tests, testing the backup and recovery process, and analyzing security incident reports.

By implementing a layered defense, organizations can create a strong defense against a variety of threats. It's important to assess the risks and vulnerabilities of your organization's information assets and select the appropriate security controls to mitigate those risks. A layered defense approach provides a comprehensive security posture that is more resilient and effective than relying on a single control.

Regularly Monitor and Test Your Security Controls

Regularly monitoring and testing your security controls is crucial for maintaining an effective security posture. Here are some steps to follow when monitoring and testing your security controls:

1. Develop a Monitoring and Testing Plan:
2. Develop a plan that outlines how you will monitor and test your security controls. This includes identifying which controls will be monitored and tested, how often they will be monitored and tested, and who will be responsible for performing the monitoring and testing.
3. Implement Automated Monitoring:
4. Implement automated monitoring tools, such as intrusion detection and prevention systems (IDS/IPS) and security information and event management (SIEM) systems, to continuously monitor your organization's network and systems for suspicious activity.
5. Conduct Regular Vulnerability Scans:
6. Conduct regular vulnerability scans to identify weaknesses in your infrastructure, such as outdated software, weak passwords, and unsecured network connections. Use the

results of these scans to prioritize remediation efforts and address vulnerabilities promptly.

7. Perform Regular Penetration Tests:

8. Perform regular penetration tests to identify how attackers could potentially exploit vulnerabilities in your infrastructure. This involves simulating a real-world attack and attempting to breach your organization's security defenses. Use the results of these tests to identify weaknesses and improve your security posture.

9. Test Backup and Recovery Processes:

10. Test your backup and recovery processes regularly to ensure that your organization's critical data can be recovered in the event of a security incident. This includes testing the backup and recovery process for all types of data, such as databases, applications, and configurations.

11. Analyze Security Incident Reports:

12. Analyze security incident reports to identify patterns and trends in security incidents. Use this information to improve your security controls and identify areas that require additional attention.

13. Continuously Improve:

14. Continuously improve your security controls based on the results of your monitoring and testing efforts. This includes addressing vulnerabilities promptly, implementing new security controls, and training employees on security best practices.

By regularly monitoring and testing your security controls, you can identify weaknesses in your infrastructure and improve your security posture. It's important to develop a plan, use automated tools, conduct regular vulnerability scans and penetration tests, test backup and recovery processes, analyze security incident reports, and continuously improve your security controls.

Define Roles and Responsibilities

Defining roles and responsibilities is an essential step in ensuring that everyone in the organization understands their responsibilities when it comes to information security. Here are some steps to follow when defining roles and responsibilities:

1. Identify Key Stakeholders:
2. Identify the key stakeholders who will be responsible for information security in your organization. This includes management, employees, contractors, and partners.
3. Develop a Governance Framework:
4. Develop a governance framework that outlines the roles and responsibilities of each stakeholder in your organization. This includes identifying who is responsible for developing security policies and procedures, implementing security controls, and monitoring and testing security controls.
5. Assign Roles and Responsibilities:
6. Assign roles and responsibilities to each stakeholder based on their expertise, job functions, and access to sensitive data. For example, the IT department may be responsible for implementing and maintaining technical security controls, while the HR department may be responsible for providing security awareness training to employees.
7. Communicate Roles and Responsibilities:
8. Communicate the roles and responsibilities to each stake-

holder in the organization. This includes providing clear guidance on what is expected of them and the consequences of failing to adhere to the security policies and procedures.

9. Provide Training and Support:
10. Provide training and support to stakeholders to ensure that they understand their roles and responsibilities and have the knowledge and skills to perform them effectively. This includes providing security awareness training, technical training, and ongoing support.
11. Review and Update Roles and Responsibilities:
12. Regularly review and update the roles and responsibilities to ensure that they remain effective and relevant to your organization's changing needs. This includes reviewing them after security incidents, changes to the regulatory environment, and major changes to your organization's infrastructure.

By defining roles and responsibilities, organizations can establish a clear accountability framework that ensures everyone understands their responsibilities and is working towards a common goal of protecting sensitive data. This can help reduce the risk of a security incident and ensure compliance with relevant regulations and standards.

Provide Security Awareness Training

Providing security awareness training is crucial for ensuring that everyone in the organization understands the importance of information security and how to protect sensitive data. Here are some steps to follow when providing security awareness training:

1. Identify Training Needs:
2. Start by identifying the training needs of your organization. This includes determining who needs training, what topics need to be covered, and how frequently training should be provided.
3. Develop a Training Program:
4. Develop a comprehensive training program that covers all the relevant security topics, such as password security, phishing scams, and social engineering. This can include in-person training sessions, online courses, and interactive workshops.
5. Customize Training to Roles:
6. Customize the training program to the roles and responsibilities of each employee. For example, employees who handle sensitive data may require more in-depth training than those who do not.
7. Provide Real-World Scenarios:
8. Provide real-world scenarios to help employees understand the impact of security incidents and the consequences of failing to follow security policies and procedures.
9. Encourage Reporting of Incidents:
10. Encourage employees to report security incidents and suspicious activity promptly. Provide clear guidance on how to report incidents and ensure that employees understand that reporting incidents is a crucial part of maintaining a secure environment.
11. Provide Ongoing Training:
12. Provide ongoing training to ensure that employees remain

up-to-date on the latest security threats and best practices. This can include regular security awareness campaigns, refresher courses, and updates to policies and procedures.

13. Measure the Effectiveness of Training:
14. Measure the effectiveness of the training program through regular evaluations and feedback from employees. Use this information to improve the training program and ensure that it remains effective.

By providing security awareness training, organizations can establish a strong security culture and reduce the risk of a security incident. It's important to identify the training needs of your organization, develop a comprehensive training program, customize training to roles, provide real-world scenarios, encourage reporting of incidents, provide ongoing training, and measure the effectiveness of the training program.

Stay Up-to-Date on Security Threats and Trends

Staying up-to-date on the latest security threats and trends is crucial for maintaining an effective security posture. Here are some steps to follow when staying up-to-date on security threats and trends:

1. Follow Industry News:
2. Stay informed about the latest security threats and trends by following industry news sources, such as security blogs, online magazines, and social media accounts.
3. Attend Security Conferences:
4. Attend security conferences and training sessions to learn about new security technologies and best practices. This

includes attending both virtual and in-person events.

5. Participate in Information Sharing:
6. Participate in information sharing programs, such as Information Sharing and Analysis Centers (ISACs) or Threat Intelligence Platforms (TIPs), to exchange information with other organizations about security threats and incidents.
7. Join Professional Associations:
8. Join professional associations, such as the Information Systems Security Association (ISSA) or the International Association of Computer Security Professionals (IACSP), to network with other security professionals and stay up-to-date on industry trends.
9. Perform Regular Threat Assessments:
10. Perform regular threat assessments to identify emerging threats and assess their potential impact on your organization's information assets. Use this information to adjust your security controls accordingly.
11. Engage with Vendors:
12. Engage with security vendors and consultants to understand the latest security technologies and how they can be applied to your organization's security program.
13. Develop a Continuous Improvement Plan:
14. Develop a continuous improvement plan that outlines how you will stay up-to-date on security threats and trends. This includes identifying who will be responsible for monitoring industry news and attending security conferences, as well as how often assessments will be performed.

By staying up-to-date on security threats and trends, organizations can stay ahead of emerging threats and maintain an effective security posture. It's important to follow industry news, attend security conferences, participate in information sharing, join professional associations, perform regular threat assessments, engage with vendors, and develop a continuous improvement plan.

Discussion

Relying on a single security control can create a single point of failure, making it easier for attackers to exploit weaknesses in your infrastructure. To ensure that security controls remain effective in a constantly evolving threat landscape, regular monitoring and testing of security controls and staying up-to-date on the latest security threats and trends is crucial.

Access control is important because it limits access to sensitive data to only those who need it, reducing the risk of data breaches and unauthorized access. Physical controls, such as security cameras, access control systems, and secure storage areas, can help prevent unauthorized access to physical spaces where sensitive information is stored. Encryption is an important security control for protecting data at rest and in transit because it helps ensure that sensitive data cannot be read by unauthorized parties.

A layered defense approach involves implementing multiple security controls to protect information assets, which can provide a more resilient and effective security posture. Security policies and procedures provide clear guidance on how to handle sensitive data and what is expected of employees, which can help create a culture of security. Security awareness training is important for all employees, regardless of their role in the organization, to ensure that all employees understand the importance of information security and how to protect sensitive data, reducing the risk of insider threats and human error.

Incident response and disaster recovery plans provide clear guidance on how to respond to security incidents and ensure that critical systems and data can be recovered quickly. Third-party vendors and contractors can have access to sensitive data and systems, so it's important to have a clear policy on how they are vetted and managed and ensure that they follow your organization's security policies and procedures.

Quiz (Solutions in Appendix)

1. What are the risks associated with relying on a single security control?
2. How can you ensure that your security controls remain effective in a constantly evolving threat landscape?
3. Why is access control such an important security control?
4. How can physical controls help protect sensitive information?
5. Why is encryption an important security control for protecting data at rest and in transit?
6. What are the benefits of implementing a layered defense approach to information security?
7. How can security policies and procedures help promote a culture of security in the organization?
8. Why is security awareness training important for all employees, regardless of their role in the organization?
9. How can incident response and disaster recovery plans

help mitigate the impact of security incidents?
10. What role do third-party vendors and contractors play in information security, and how can you ensure that they follow your organization's security policies and procedures?

6

Information Security Laws and Standards

Information security laws and standards are designed to protect the confidentiality, integrity, and availability of information in various settings, such as government, healthcare, finance, and e-commerce. These laws and standards establish best practices for organizations to follow in order to safeguard their sensitive information and prevent unauthorized access, use, or disclosure. Here are some commonly recognized information security laws and standards:

1. General Data Protection Regulation (GDPR): A regulation in the European Union that sets out rules for the processing and storage of personal data.
2. Health Insurance Portability and Accountability Act (HIPAA): A U.S. law that requires healthcare providers to safeguard the privacy and security of patients' medical information.
3. Payment Card Industry Data Security Standard (PCI DSS): A set of requirements for any organization that handles

credit card information to ensure that sensitive data is protected against fraud.

4. ISO 27001: A widely recognized international standard for information security management systems (ISMS) that specifies a framework for implementing and maintaining effective security controls.

5. Federal Information Security Management Act (FISMA): A U.S. law that requires federal agencies to develop, implement, and maintain information security programs to protect government information and systems.

6. Sarbanes-Oxley Act (SOX): A U.S. law that requires companies to maintain accurate financial reporting and internal controls to prevent fraud.

7. NIST Cybersecurity Framework: A voluntary framework created by the National Institute of Standards and Technology (NIST) to help organizations manage and reduce cybersecurity risks.

Compliance with these laws and standards is crucial for organizations to protect their data, maintain the trust of their customers, and avoid legal and financial consequences resulting from data breaches or noncompliance.

Information security standards

Information security standards provide guidelines, best practices, and requirements for organizations to manage and protect their information assets. Here are two widely recognized information security standards:

1. ISO 27001: ISO 27001 is an internationally recognized

standard for information security management systems (ISMS). The standard provides a framework for organizations to establish, implement, maintain, and continually improve an ISMS, which is a systematic approach to managing sensitive company information. The standard outlines a set of controls that organizations can use to manage risks related to information security. ISO 27001 also provides a process-based approach to risk management that emphasizes continuous improvement, as well as a set of requirements that organizations must meet to achieve certification.

2. NIST Cybersecurity Framework: The NIST Cybersecurity Framework is a voluntary framework developed by the National Institute of Standards and Technology (NIST) to help organizations manage and reduce cybersecurity risks. The framework provides a set of guidelines, best practices, and standards to help organizations identify, assess, and manage cybersecurity risks. The framework is organized around five core functions: Identify, Protect, Detect, Respond, and Recover. Each function includes a set of categories and subcategories that provide more specific guidance on how to implement cybersecurity best practices.

Both ISO 27001 and the NIST Cybersecurity Framework provide a framework for organizations to manage and reduce cybersecurity risks. While ISO 27001 focuses specifically on information security management systems, the NIST Cybersecurity Framework is more broadly applicable to all types of organizations. Both standards emphasize the importance of continuous improvement, risk management, and compliance with best practices and requirements to ensure the confiden-tiality, integrity, and availability of sensitive information.

Compliance

Compliance with information security laws and standards is essential for organizations to protect their information assets and maintain the trust of their customers. Here are some reasons why compliance is important:

1. Legal and regulatory requirements: Noncompliance with information security laws and standards can result in legal and regulatory consequences, such as fines, penalties, and legal liability. For example, the General Data Protection Regulation (GDPR) includes fines of up to 4% of a com-pany's global revenue for noncompliance.
2. Protection of sensitive data: Information security laws and standards help organizations protect their sensitive data from unauthorized access, use, and disclosure. Compli-ance with these standards can help prevent data breaches and mitigate the potential impact of a breach on the organization and its customers.
3. Trust and reputation: Compliance with information secu-rity laws and standards can help build and maintain trust with customers, partners, and stakeholders. Organizations that demonstrate a commitment to information security through compliance are more likely to be seen as trustwor-thy and reliable.
4. Competitive advantage: Compliance with information security laws and standards can provide a competitive advantage by demonstrating a higher level of security and

reliability compared to competitors who do not comply with these standards.

5. Continuous improvement: Compliance with information security laws and standards encourages organizations to adopt best practices and continually improve their security posture. This can help organizations stay ahead of evolving threats and risks and better protect their sensitive data.

In summary, compliance with information security laws and standards is critical for organizations to protect their sensitive data, maintain the trust of their customers, and avoid legal and financial consequences resulting from noncompliance.

Legal and regulatory requirements

Legal and regulatory requirements related to information security vary by country and industry. Here are some examples of information security laws and regulations that organizations may need to comply with:

1. General Data Protection Regulation (GDPR): A regulation in the European Union that sets out rules for the processing and storage of personal data.
2. Health Insurance Portability and Accountability Act (HIPAA): A U.S. law that requires healthcare providers to safeguard the privacy and security of patients' medical information.
3. Payment Card Industry Data Security Standard (PCI DSS): A set of requirements for any organization that handles credit card information to ensure that sensitive data is protected against fraud.

4. Sarbanes-Oxley Act (SOX): A U.S. law that requires companies to maintain accurate financial reporting and internal controls to prevent fraud.

5. Federal Information Security Modernization Act (FISMA): A U.S. law that requires federal agencies to develop, implement, and maintain information security programs to protect government information and systems.

6. Cybersecurity Information Sharing Act (CISA): A U.S. law that encourages private sector companies to share cybersecurity threat information with the federal government to enhance the overall cybersecurity posture of the country.

7. Personal Information Protection and Electronic Documents Act (PIPEDA): A Canadian law that sets out rules for the collection, use, and disclosure of personal information by private sector organizations.

Compliance with these laws and regulations is essential to protect sensitive information, maintain the trust of customers, and avoid legal and financial consequences resulting from data breaches or noncompliance. Organizations must understand the specific requirements and regulations that apply to their industry and location and implement appropriate measures to comply with them.

Protection of sensitive data

Protecting sensitive data is a critical aspect of information security. Sensitive data can include personally identifiable information (PII), financial data, health information, intellectual property, and other types of confidential information. Here are some ways organizations can protect sensitive data:

1. Encryption: Encryption is a process of converting plain text data into an unreadable form that can only be deciphered with a secret key. Encryption can protect data both at rest (stored on a device or server) and in transit (being transmitted over a network).

2. Access controls: Access controls are security mechanisms that restrict access to sensitive data to authorized personnel only. Access controls can include password policies, multi-factor authentication, and role-based access controls.

3. Data classification: Data classification is a process of categorizing data according to its level of sensitivity, value, and criticality. This can help organizations apply appropriate security controls to protect sensitive data and ensure that it is handled appropriately.

4. Data minimization: Data minimization is a practice of collecting and storing only the minimum amount of data necessary to accomplish a specific purpose. This can help reduce the risk of data breaches and limit the amount of sensitive data that is exposed in case of a breach.

5. Data backup and recovery: Regular data backups can help ensure that sensitive data is not lost in case of a breach or system failure. Organizations should also have a plan in place for recovering from a data breach or other security incident.

6. Employee training and awareness: Employees are often the weakest link in information security. Organizations should provide regular training and awareness programs to help employees understand the importance of protecting sensitive data and how to do so effectively.

In summary, protecting sensitive data is essential to maintaining information security. Organizations should implement appropriate security measures such as encryption, access controls, data classification, and data minimization to protect sensitive data from unauthorized access, use, or disclosure. Additionally, regular employee training and awareness programs can help ensure that everyone in the organization understands the importance of protecting sensitive data.

Trust and reputation

Trust and reputation are essential for the success of any organization, and information security plays a critical role in building and maintaining that trust. Here are some ways that information security can impact an organization's trust and reputation:

1. Customer confidence: Customers are more likely to do business with organizations that they trust to protect their sensitive data. Compliance with information security laws and standards can help demonstrate an organization's commitment to protecting customer data and maintain their confidence.
2. Brand reputation: A data breach or other security incident can damage an organization's brand reputation and erode customer trust. Implementing strong information security measures and responding quickly and effectively to security incidents can help mitigate the impact on an organization's reputation.
3. Competitive advantage: Organizations that can demonstrate a higher level of information security than their

competitors can gain a competitive advantage by building customer trust and confidence.

4. Regulatory compliance: Compliance with information security laws and regulations is essential to avoid legal and financial consequences resulting from noncompliance. Compliance can help demonstrate an organization's commitment to ethical business practices and build trust with regulators and stakeholders.

5. Employee morale: Employees who feel that their organization takes information security seriously are more likely to be satisfied and engaged in their work. This can improve productivity and reduce turnover.

In summary, information security plays a critical role in building and maintaining trust and reputation. Organizations that prioritize information security and comply with relevant laws and standards can build customer confidence, enhance their brand reputation, gain a competitive advantage, and improve employee morale.

Competitive advantage

Information security can provide a competitive advantage to organizations in several ways. Here are some examples:

1. Customer trust: Organizations that can demonstrate a higher level of information security can build trust with their customers, which can result in increased customer loyalty and retention.

2. Compliance: Compliance with information security laws and regulations can help organizations avoid legal and

financial consequences resulting from noncompliance. Compliance can also help organizations demonstrate their commitment to ethical business practices, which can be an important factor for customers when making purchasing decisions.

3. Reputation: A strong information security posture can enhance an organization's reputation and brand image, which can help attract new customers and retain existing ones. Organizations that are perceived as trustworthy and reliable are more likely to be successful in competitive markets.

4. Competitive differentiation: Information security can be a key differentiator in competitive markets, especially in industries where customers are particularly sensitive about the protection of their data, such as healthcare, finance, and e-commerce. Organizations that can demonstrate a higher level of information security can set themselves apart from their competitors and gain a competitive advantage.

5. Cost savings: Implementing effective information security measures can help organizations avoid the costs associated with data breaches and other security incidents. This can result in cost savings that can be reinvested in other areas of the organization, such as research and development, marketing, or customer service.

In summary, information security can provide a competitive advantage to organizations by building customer trust, ensuring compliance, enhancing reputation, differentiating from competitors, and reducing costs associated with security incidents.

Continuous improvement

Continuous improvement is a critical aspect of information security management. Cybersecurity threats and risks are constantly evolving, and organizations must adapt and improve their security posture to stay ahead of the curve. Here are some ways organizations can continually improve their information security:

1. Risk management: Organizations should regularly assess and manage their cybersecurity risks. Risk assessments can help identify vulnerabilities and prioritize security measures based on the potential impact of a security incident.
2. Training and awareness: Employees are often the weakest link in information security. Regular training and awareness programs can help employees understand the importance of information security and how to protect sensitive data effectively.
3. Incident response planning: Organizations should have a plan in place for responding to security incidents. Incident response planning can help minimize the impact of a security incident and enable the organization to recover more quickly.
4. Technology updates: Organizations should regularly update their technology, including software, hardware, and infrastructure, to ensure that they are using the latest security features and patches.
5. Third-party risk management: Many organizations rely on third-party vendors for critical business functions. Organizations should have processes in place to manage third-

party risks and ensure that vendors are complying with relevant information security standards and requirements.

6. Continuous monitoring: Organizations should continuously monitor their networks and systems for security incidents. Monitoring can help detect and respond to security incidents more quickly and minimize the potential impact of a breach.

In summary, continuous improvement is essential to maintaining an effective information security management program. Organizations should regularly assess and manage risks, provide training and awareness programs, have an incident response plan in place, regularly update technology, manage third-party risks, and continuously monitor networks and systems. By continually improving their information security, organizations can reduce the risk of data breaches and other security incidents and maintain the trust of their customers.

Discussion

Compliance with information security laws and standards is crucial for organizations to avoid legal and regulatory consequences. Noncompliance can result in fines, penalties, legal liability, and reputational damage. Moreover, customers may lose their trust in an organization that fails to comply with relevant laws and standards. Organizations must continually improve their information security management systems as cybersecurity threats and risks are constantly evolving. This continuous improvement requires monitoring, evaluation, and modification of security measures.

Information security standards, such as ISO 27001, NIST Cyber-security Framework, and PCI DSS, differ in their requirements and implementation. For example, ISO 27001 is a globally recognized standard for information security management, while the NIST Cybersecurity Framework is a voluntary framework for improving critical infrastructure cybersecurity. PCI DSS is a set of requirements for organizations that handle credit card information to ensure the protection of sensitive data against fraud.

Compliance with information security laws and standards can provide several benefits to organizations, including protecting sensitive data, maintaining customer trust, providing a competitive advantage, and avoiding legal and financial consequences resulting from noncompliance. Organizations can manage third-party risks related to information security by establishing vendor management processes, conducting due diligence on vendors, and ensuring that vendors comply with relevant information security standards and requirements.

Effective incident response planning is essential to minimize the impact of a security incident and enable the organization to recover quickly. Best practices for incident response planning include developing a clear incident response plan, identifying and training incident response teams, regularly testing the plan, and continuously improving the plan based on lessons learned.

Challenges organizations may face when implementing information security laws and standards include a lack of resources, expertise, and resistance to change. Organizations can ensure that their employees are aware of information security risks and best practices by providing regular training and awareness programs, using phishing simulations, and enforcing policies and procedures related to information security.

The key elements of an effective information security management system include risk management, policy and procedure development, access controls, incident response planning, and continuous improvement. Organizations can ensure that they are complying with relevant information security laws and standards by conducting regular audits, performing risk assessments, and seeking certification from third-party auditors.

Quiz (Solutions in Appendix)

1. What are the potential consequences of noncompliance with information security laws and standards?
2. Why is continuous improvement important in information security management?
3. What are some common information security standards and how do they differ?
4. What are the benefits of complying with information security laws and standards?
5. How can organizations manage third-party risks related to information security?
6. What are some best practices for incident response planning in information security?
7. What are some challenges organizations face when implementing information security laws and standards?
8. How can organizations ensure that their employees are aware of information security risks and best practices?
9. What are the key elements of an effective information

security management system?

10. How can organizations ensure that they are complying with relevant information security laws and standards?

If you've read my book

If you've read my book, I would be grateful if you could take a moment to leave an honest review on Amazon. Your review will not only help other readers make an informed decision but also provide valuable feedback to me as an author. Thank you for taking the time to share your thoughts!

Information Security Overview Quiz Solutions

What are the most common types of information security threats?

Answer: The most common types of information security threats include malware, phishing, insider threats, denial of service (DoS) attacks, advanced persistent threats (APTs), man-in-the-middle (MitM) attacks, physical attacks, and data breaches.

How can organizations protect against information security threats?

Answer: Organizations can protect against information security threats by implementing strong security protocols, such as access controls, encryption, and regular security training for employees. They can also use intrusion detection and prevention systems, firewalls, and other tools to monitor and protect their networks and systems.

What are the potential consequences of a data breach?

Answer: A data breach can result in financial loss, reputation damage, legal and regulatory penalties, disruption of operations, and personal harm to individuals whose data has been exposed.

What is the impact of insider threats on organizations?

Answer: Insider threats can have a significant impact on organizations, including loss of intellectual property, reputational damage, financial loss, and legal and regulatory penalties.

How can individuals protect themselves from information security threats?

Answer: Individuals can protect themselves from information security threats by being vigilant about phishing scams, using strong passwords and two-factor authentication, keeping their software up-to-date, and avoiding public Wi-Fi networks when accessing sensitive data.

What are some emerging information security threats?

Answer: Emerging information security threats include artificial intelligence (AI)-powered attacks, ransomware-as-a-service (RaaS), and attacks targeting Internet of Things (IoT) devices.

How can organizations balance the need for data security with the need for data accessibility?

Answer: Organizations can balance the need for data security with the need for data accessibility by implementing strong access controls, using encryption and other security measures to protect sensitive data, and providing access to data only to those who need it.

What is the role of government in protecting against information security threats?

Answer: Governments play a role in protecting against information security threats by passing and enforcing data protection laws, sharing threat intelligence with other countries and organizations, and investing in cybersecurity research and development.

How can organizations prepare for a cybersecurity incident?

Answer: Organizations can prepare for a cybersecurity incident by developing a comprehensive incident response plan, conducting regular security assessments and penetration testing, and providing regular security training to employees.

What are the ethical implications of using personal data for cybersecurity purposes?

Answer: The use of personal data for cybersecurity purposes raises ethical concerns, including issues of privacy, consent, and the potential for misuse of personal data. It is important for organizations to use personal data responsibly and transparently, and to comply with relevant data protection laws and regulations.

Cyber Kill Chain Concepts Quiz Solutions

How can organizations detect and prevent attacks that do not follow the traditional Cyber Kill Chain model?

One solution could be to implement machine learning algorithms and behavioral analysis tools that can detect unusual activity and identify anomalies that may indicate an attack.

What role can individuals play in preventing cyber attacks that target their personal devices and data?

One solution could be to educate individuals about cyber hygiene and best practices, such as using strong passwords, enabling two-factor authentication, and avoiding suspicious links and attachments.

How can organizations ensure that their employees are aware of the threats posed by social engineering attacks, and how can they train them to recognize and avoid these attacks?

One solution could be to provide regular security awareness training that includes simulated phishing attacks and other social engineering scenarios.

What can organizations do to prevent cyber attacks from insider threats, such as employees with malicious intent or those who unintentionally compromise security?

One solution could be to implement access controls, monitoring tools, and background checks to prevent unauthorized access and to detect suspicious activity.

How can organizations improve incident response and reduce the time to detect and respond to cyber attacks?

One solution could be to implement a security operations center (SOC) and incident response team that can quickly detect and respond to security incidents.

What role can threat intelligence play in helping organizations identify and prevent cyber attacks before they happen?

One solution could be to implement threat intelligence feeds that provide real-time information about emerging threats and vulnerabilities.

How can organizations ensure that their security controls are effective and up-to-date, given the constantly evolving nature of cyber threats?

One solution could be to conduct regular security assessments and penetration testing to identify vulnerabilities and assess the effectiveness of security controls.

What can organizations do to ensure that their supply chain

partners and third-party vendors are not compromising their security?

One solution could be to implement a third-party risk management program that includes due diligence and ongoing monitoring of supply chain partners and vendors.

How can organizations prevent data exfiltration and ensure the security of their sensitive data, even in the event of a successful cyber attack?

One solution could be to implement strong data encryption, access controls, and data loss prevention tools.

What role can governments and international organizations play in promoting global cybersecurity and preventing cyber attacks on critical infrastructure and other important targets?

One solution could be to establish international norms and agreements that promote responsible behavior in cyberspace, and to improve international cooperation and information sharing to detect and prevent cyber attacks.

Hacking Concepts Quiz Solutions

How can organizations strike a balance between providing accessibility to their systems while also securing them against hacking attempts?

Solution: Organizations can implement multi-factor authentication, regularly update software and security systems, and provide regular security training to employees.

What ethical considerations should white hat hackers take into account when identifying and disclosing vulnerabilities in systems?

Solution: White hat hackers should always follow responsible disclosure practices and work with system owners to patch vulnerabilities before making them public.

How can individuals protect themselves from phishing attacks and other forms of social engineering?

Solution: Individuals can be cautious when clicking on links or downloading attachments from unknown sources, use strong passwords, and be aware of the potential risks of sharing sensitive information online.

How can software developers create more secure applications and systems?

Solution: Developers can use secure coding practices, such as input validation and parameterized queries, and regularly test their applications for vulnerabilities.

How can law enforcement and government agencies effectively combat cybercrime and hacking?

Solution: Law enforcement and government agencies can work with international partners, implement strong cybersecurity policies, and provide education and resources to the public.

What are the potential consequences of a successful hacking attempt on critical infrastructure systems, such as power grids or transportation networks?

Solution: The consequences of a successful hacking attempt on critical infrastructure systems can be severe, including power outages, transportation disruptions, and financial losses.

How can individuals and organizations protect themselves against ransomware attacks?

Solution: Individuals and organizations can use anti-virus and anti-malware software, regularly update software and security systems, and back up important data regularly.

What impact has the proliferation of the Internet of Things (IoT) had on cybersecurity, and what steps can be taken to mitigate the risks?

Solution: The growth of IoT has created new vulnerabilities and attack vectors, and organizations and individuals should implement strong security measures, such as network segmentation and strong authentication protocols.

How can individuals and organizations protect their sensitive data from being stolen by hackers?

Solution: Individuals and organizations can use strong passwords, encryption, and two-factor authentication to protect their sensitive data from being stolen by hackers.

How can the public and private sectors work together to improve overall cybersecurity and reduce the risk of hacking attempts?

Solution: Public-private partnerships can involve information sharing, joint exercises and training, and collaboration on cybersecurity policy and regulation.

Ethical Hacking Concepts Quiz Solutions

What are some ethical considerations that ethical hackers must take into account when performing a penetration test?

Answer: Ethical hackers must obtain permission from the system or network owner, adhere to the terms of the testing agreement, and ensure that the testing process does not cause any harm to the target system or network.

What are some of the most common vulnerabilities that ethical hackers identify during the testing process?

Answer: Common vulnerabilities include outdated software versions, weak passwords, misconfigured systems, and open network shares.

How can ethical hacking help organizations to improve their cybersecurity posture?

Answer: Ethical hacking can help organizations identify potential vulnerabilities in their systems and networks, and provide recommendations for remediation to improve their security posture.

What are some of the ethical implications of using social engineering techniques during an ethical hacking test?

Answer: Social engineering techniques can be used to obtain sensitive information from individuals, which could violate their privacy. Ethical hackers must ensure that these techniques are used within acceptable ethical boundaries.

How does ethical hacking differ from malicious hacking?

Answer: Ethical hacking is performed with the permission of the system or network owner, and is focused on identifying vulnerabilities for the purpose of improving security. Malicious hacking is performed without permission, and is focused on causing harm to the target system or network.

What are some of the legal considerations that ethical hackers must take into account during the testing process?

Answer: Ethical hackers must ensure that the testing process does not violate any laws or regulations, and must obtain the necessary permissions and waivers before performing any testing.

How do ethical hackers keep their skills up-to-date and stay informed about new threats and vulnerabilities?

Answer: Ethical hackers can attend training courses, conferences, and webinars, and can participate in online communities to stay informed about new threats and vulnerabilities.

How can ethical hacking be used to test the security of cloud-based systems and applications?

Answer: Ethical hacking can be used to identify potential vulnerabilities in cloud-based systems and applications, and can provide recommendations for remediation to improve their security posture.

What are some of the challenges that ethical hackers may face during the testing process?

Answer: Ethical hackers may face challenges such as unresponsive system owners, limited access to resources, and new and emerging threats and vulnerabilities.

How can organizations use the results of an ethical hacking test to improve their overall security posture?

Answer: Organizations can use the results of an ethical hacking test to identify potential vulnerabilities and weaknesses in their systems and networks, and to develop a plan for remediation to improve their overall security posture.

Information Security Laws and Standards Quiz Solutions

What are the potential consequences of noncompliance with information security laws and standards?

Answer: Noncompliance with information security laws and standards can result in legal and regulatory consequences, such as fines, penalties, and legal liability. It can also damage an organization's reputation and erode customer trust.

Why is continuous improvement important in information security management?

Answer: Continuous improvement is important in information security management because cybersecurity threats and risks are constantly evolving, and organizations must adapt and improve their security posture to stay ahead of the curve.

What are some common information security standards and how do they differ?

Answer: Some common information security standards include ISO 27001, NIST Cybersecurity Framework, and PCI DSS. These standards differ in their scope, requirements, and implementation.

What are the benefits of complying with information security laws and standards?

Answer: Complying with information security laws and standards can help protect sensitive data, maintain the trust of customers, provide a competitive advantage, and avoid legal and financial consequences resulting from noncompliance.

How can organizations manage third-party risks related to information security?

Answer: Organizations can manage third-party risks related to information security by establishing vendor management processes, conducting due diligence on vendors, and ensuring that vendors comply with relevant information security standards and requirements.

What are some best practices for incident response planning in information security?

Answer: Some best practices for incident response planning in information security include developing a clear incident response plan, identifying and training incident response teams, regularly testing the plan, and continuously improving the plan based on lessons learned.

What are some challenges organizations face when implementing information security laws and standards?

Answer: Some challenges organizations face when implementing information security laws and standards include lack of resources, lack of expertise, and resistance to change.

How can organizations ensure that their employees are aware of information security risks and best practices?

Answer: Organizations can ensure that their employees are aware of information security risks and best practices by providing regular training and awareness programs, using phishing simulations, and enforcing policies and procedures related to information security.

What are the key elements of an effective information security management system?

Answer: The key elements of an effective information security management system include risk management, policy and procedure development, access controls, incident response planning, and continuous improvement.

How can organizations ensure that they are complying with relevant information security laws and standards?

Answer: Organizations can ensure that they are complying with relevant information security laws and standards by conducting regular audits, performing risk assessments, and seeking certification from third-party auditors.

Information Security Controls Quiz Solutions

What are the risks associated with relying on a single security control?

Answer: Relying on a single security control can create a single point of failure, making it easier for attackers to exploit weaknesses in your infrastructure.

How can you ensure that your security controls remain effective in a constantly evolving threat landscape?

Answer: Regularly monitoring and testing your security controls and staying up-to-date on the latest security threats and trends can help ensure that your security controls remain effective.

Why is access control such an important security control?

Answer: Access control is important because it limits access to sensitive data to only those who need it, reducing the risk of data breaches and unauthorized access.

How can physical controls help protect sensitive information?

Answer: Physical controls, such as security cameras, access control systems, and secure storage areas, can help prevent unauthorized access to physical spaces where sensitive information is stored.

Why is encryption an important security control for protecting data at rest and in transit?

Answer: Encryption helps ensure that sensitive data cannot be read by unauthorized parties, even if it is intercepted during transit or stolen from a storage device.

What are the benefits of implementing a layered defense approach to information security?

Answer: A layered defense approach involves implementing multiple security controls to protect information assets, which can provide a more resilient and effective security posture.

How can security policies and procedures help promote a culture of security in the organization?

Answer: Security policies and procedures provide clear guidance on how to handle sensitive data and what is expected of employees, which can help create a culture of security.

Why is security awareness training important for all employees, regardless of their role in the organization?

Answer: Security awareness training helps ensure that all employees understand the importance of information security and how to protect sensitive data, reducing the risk of insider threats and human error.

How can incident response and disaster recovery plans help mitigate the impact of security incidents?

Answer: Incident response and disaster recovery plans provide clear guidance on how to respond to security incidents and ensure that critical systems and data can be recovered quickly.

What role do third-party vendors and contractors play in information security, and how can you ensure that they follow your organization's security policies and procedures?

Answer: Third-party vendors and contractors can have access to sensitive data and systems, so it's important to have a clear policy on how they are vetted and managed, and to ensure that they follow your organization's security policies and procedures.

www.ingramcontent.com/pod-product-compliance
Lightning Source LLC
LaVergne TN
LVHW051700050326
832903LV00032B/3926